A soldier has his rifle,
a knight has his sword,
an archer has his bow,
and an author has his book.

Lies I Never Quite Believed

The Emancipation of Akil Johnson

Written and Arranged
By Akil Johnson

Edited By Jimmy

Lies I Never Quite Believed
The Emancipation of Akil Johnson

Copyright © 2012 Akil Johnson
Published by ApoeticLife Publishing

ISBN: 978-0-9856055-0-6

Printed in the United States of America

Contents

❦ Dedication ❦

To the precious souls like me who too once lost their way
Every word I've written here you've inspired me to say
Take this book as my love letter to each of you
Because of your faith in me
I know what faith can do

Introduction

"This little light of mine,
I'm gonna let it shine.
This little light of mine,
I'm gonna let it shine.
This little light of mine,
I'm gonna let it shine...
Let it shine,
Let it shine,
Let it shine."

I grew up in church singing this song in the company of the saints. But it was in the company of the people who saints would call sinners, that I would truly learn what those words actually meant. That moment in 1995, found me sitting in the auditorium of the Whitelaw Reid JHS 57 in Brooklyn New York. Our principal, Mr. Robert Norris, had called a school-wide meeting once again. We all wondered who was in trouble this time. JHS 57 was filled with many troubled youths, who lived in surrounding areas riddled with crime. It was the kind of neighborhood where you just never knew what day might be your day to see the ugliness come your way. Mr. Norris had arrived onto the auditorium stage, standing where he had stood many a time. A student had written the anonymous letter in his hand. In it, he said, there were some things he hoped we would come to understand. We all wondered what could be so special about this letter as he read:

> *"Dear Mr. Norris," he said, "Oh do we have a school or do we have a place where all the children rule, Oh no, let's take action, let's not let them rule. Let's exercise our right to have a better school.".*

As he read on, for there was so much more to read, I saw thousands of my fellow students erupt in a mixture of emotions inspired by that seed. Something special was taking place, something I saw the evidence of on each students' face. It was the moment I first knew, what the power of words could do. They could be a light in our darkest hour, turning our pain into power. No one knew the author of the letter Mr. Norris read that day. Except for the teacher who delivered it and swore she would never say. I couldn't risk standing and addressing the crowd, but there I sat terrified hoping that no one would ever find out that those were my thoughts being read out loud.

Anonymity was the only option to insure my safety in the very hostile environment that inspired all the things I felt I had to say, as the author of the letter Mr. Norris read on that fateful day.

That day would mark the beginning of many good things. It was when God turned up the fire that would burn deep within me, enabling me to face the many challenging situations I'd experience over time. He knew that in a world of lies, it would often be the only truth I'd find. *"Lies I Never Quite Believed"* is a book about the journey I've been on for the last 30 years. It's my story told through childhood experiences and a series of articles I've been inspired to write through those years. It represents a literary map of the road to my personal emancipation.

A loss of innocence

As a child, I craved the love and support that all children need to help them grow into productive citizens of the world. A world we desire a certain level of acceptance from. Those of us who are fortunate, experience this first on a personal level from our families. I knew not this sense of belonging, and as a result, my need for love and acceptance led me down a path of painful experiences, which I haven't always dealt with in a productive manner.

I spent a significant part of my early childhood living with my grandparents on an island called Tortola in the

Virgin Islands. Although it was a full house, with five of my Grandparents' ten children living there, I felt utterly alone. I was the only grandchild living with them at the time, that meant I was the recipient of all the attention, not all of it welcomed, from family and friends. It was a simple life depending on which window you were looking in from, or whose eyes you were looking out through. I had many days that could be described as ordinary, like those in which I would meet my cousin Ben after school to go off on one of our adventures. We had countless days of fun that I don't recall all the details of, but I do remember them being happy, carefree days with hours of play on the bay in water, dirt and sand; or through the hills of our family's land. This was the paradise we knew on an island surrounded by seas of blue. We were proud to belong to such a wondrous place, described as "Natures Little Secret."

I am sad to say that although Ben and I had many days of play, the memories of one particular day seemed to wipe the details of all the happier ones away. One day after school on a day that wasn't so ordinary, Ben told me that his older half-sister Greta wanted us to come up by their house, which we often did anyway. I don't recall the reason he gave or if he even gave a reason, only that he seemed troubled by the task which Greta had given him. I didn't go with him on his first or second try, but on this day I felt like he needed me, although I had no way of knowing why. As we walked together I knew then, through his silence, that he had been changed, and that I was about to be changed also by the plan that had been arranged.

When we finally got there Greta was waiting. As he walked away she took me behind the house in a small dark cold space where she could hear and see anyone who might be approaching that area from a distance. I don't know if that is where my cousin Ben lost his innocence, but it was where I certainly lost mine. I measured the gravity of the experience by the guilt of my cousin who was unable to look at me, and the way in which I was then unable to look at myself.

I knew that she had molested him because those were the stories she told as she molested me. After he had threatened to tell their father, you see, she told him to find her someone else, and, for more times than I care to remember, that someone else was me. I had no words to describe the experience then, nor those that continued from that day forward to happen. I just knew on some level that I was a 7-year-old boy with a damaged identity, that was the person I saw when I looked at me. These events colored my life in ways a child should never know. There where no crayons in my box, no characters in my coloring books, for me to express on paper, how a broken child's heart looks.

While growing up in my Grandparents' house I got many answers to questions I never asked. They were answers that helped to define my then damaged identity, which was born out of my mistaken idea of me. As I learned new words to call myself I also grew to hate who I was growing up to be. I used to stand in the mirror and recite the words that would cut me open day and night, words I couldn't get out of my head, they rose with me in the morning and were still there when I went to bed. It was a collage of all the things they said, and in my quiet moments alone, I made all their words my own.

Years later while living with my Mother, my Father would come to visit from time to time on weekends, giving me the opportunity to get to know him on some level. Though the events of my young life would prevent me from ever really knowing and trusting them, I tried, but failed to forge a connection with them. They were both fleeting figures in my life at one time or another, whom I missed and loved much more than maybe I wanted to know. For it was the emptiness left in their absence that painfully told me so. I wondered if they missed me in the same way. I wondered if they felt the void I felt every minute of every day. I remember the moment I stopped feeling like a child anymore, and started feeling like someone's slutty little whore.

For reasons unknown to me, this manifested itself as anger deep inside. The more this anger became a force in my life, the more I acted out in various ways as troubled children often do. And as that anger grew, I heard my fathers name often mentioned in association with mine. He was the angry man who bore an angry son who he didn't even know, and I, the angry son who grew up wondering why this was so.

In an effort to understand me my father would ask me on several occasions throughout my childhood if I saw myself as a victim. It was a question that as a child I never really knew how to answer. What I knew was that he had no idea what I had been a victim of. He only knew what was obvious; I was distant and somewhat noncommunicative with him. I wasn't prepared to share what I'd been through with either of my parents, who, due to no fault of their own, were not there to support me while I dealt with the consequences had I done so.

A decade later due to the many circumstances that defined the reality of the time, I found myself back in the Virgin Islands in my grandparents' house. The place I swore I would never allow myself to be again, because I knew the memories there were not my friend. What was different this time around was that I had a purpose for being in this place, I had demons there, demons I needed to face. I found myself in the presence of the people with whom I had lost the natural love we have for life. The words they used as tools to abuse me and each other, could be used as tools to free me, I would soon discover.

It wasn't until I got an opportunity to write a weekly column for a popular local newspaper called the "BVI Penny Saver" that I realized words could also help inspire the community. This opportunity, which I couldn't believe was happening to me, unfortunately was not without controversy. As you can imagine most of the members of my family were not pleased at all with me, and in such a small community, which it was and still is today, everyone is family.

I don't know all the reasons why my articles became so popular, but here's what I do know: When this opportunity presented itself, my reality was not good. Like so many others, I was a teenager in great pain. And regardless of what a bloody mess of emotions my articles would be, they were an honest look at the ugly person I saw when I looked at me. But they would also serve to document the realization of the wonderful, powerful, and influential young man that I now knew I could be.

As I wrote and I grew with little support from my family, doors opened, seas parted, and I was "a public figure," "activist," "poet," suddenly. I was described in this way by prominent members of the community, which in effect, itself became all the support I would ever need. There were countless personal moments shared with people who only knew me through the colorful words they had read in black and white. They let me know that they appreciated my insight, my light, my fight. It helped me to work through all the pain, and because of these experiences I knew my quiet tears were not in vain.

The silence that was as loud as the rain on a tin roof had come to an end, in the face of a new silence that would be as cold as a northern wind. My silence as a victim had ended finally, only to be replaced by a silence from the family that was unable to protect me from the ugly truth they were unwilling to see. They read and heard the words I was speaking, but they erected a wall around the topics I was breaching. They would rarely ever mention my controversial expressions to my face, but I would feel the bitter cold of their whispered voices in my wake.

It was articles like the following that would usher in my new-found voice. As I wrote this article I knew that it would be the beginning of the book you now hold in your hands. It served as the catalyst of many things that I needed to say. So let us take a look back at some of the formative events in my life starting with the article that has led up to this present day.

The silence has just traded places

It is so important to have a voice, for what it means is that you have a choice. There are those among us who are uncomfortable when others speak, because when we raise our voice they lose the power over us which they seek. They need us to be less of a person so they can feel complete. I am here to declare today to the people in my own life who with me used to have their way that their reign has come to an end. I hope you find the strength to do the same, and to be your own best friend. Silence keeps us in so many ways, we are in relationships with people who have us so controlled we don't even know what to say. We have lost ourselves because we are too afraid to show it and we deny our own truth because we are too afraid to know it.

When I was a child I remember feeling like I would never be good enough to matter. In an environment where the belief was children should be seen and not heard. Seen and not understood, our voices muffled and our self-esteem not good. I hated the God of my grandfathers understanding, much like him, He seemed unloving and yet so demanding. A God who expected so much but gave so little, the same as my grandfather expected of me. He was like the God my young mind understood God to be. He used to say when you grow up you're going to be a sissy, one more day and you would have been a girl in your mothers' belly. When I was a child my grandfather was like God to me. I watched him preach the Gospel of Jesus Christ, but when he came home there were times where he was simply not nice. He represented a God that was disappointed in me, as family reading this now may also be.

When I was a child I fought a lot at school, instilled fear in other children because at home that's what I knew. When I was at home there was no me, so when I went to school I took away other children's identity. No one stood up for them, no one stood up for me. Who were they going to tell that this little boy was their bully? Who was I going to tell that my cousin was molesting me and that my uncle was looking at me like how guys look at girls? I learned early on that we live in a messed up world. A world who's sleeping children can hardly close their eyes, wondering who might enter their rooms and leave them compromised. I guess they got my grandfather's memo, and before I even grew up they figured they'd use me as a demo.

I once wanted to be where my grandfather is today, in a cemetery dead because I already felt that way. I'm still here though grandpa and wouldn't you be surprised to pick up the paper only to see your grandson's name capitalized. I've decided to take control of my own destiny, and to explore a potential you were not able to see. What doesn't kill you makes you stronger is not my philosophy, but I wouldn't take anything in exchange for the man I know as me. I was born into an inconvenient truth and still today I see those who came before and after me tripping over the roots. Some of us almost died while falling from the tree, then it seemed we got tied to it no more - better to be.

You know it's really not so surprising how we become our parents without realizing. We order up their mistakes, except we're super sizing. We don't have to live a lie but we have gotten so comfortable with it, the truth seems hard to try. I personally know that the price to speak it is relatively high.

I bore the scars of that inconvenient truth, now I speak the wisdom of an inconvenient youth. To me God has been incredibly good. He has been the father my grandfather never could. And to the contrary, by my side He has always stood. In many ways as a child I felt held back, when I wanted to speak I was threatened with a slap. Now like a sling shot coming back to devastate what use to be, what silence has allowed to happen in our society.

They tired to cut me out, off the newspaper page. Now as a result, I have platinum range. Excuse me while I rise again, it is good when you get to know God as your friend. The silence isn't over but it has just traded places, and this is a new day judging from the look on your faces. I choose to no longer live the silence of an unspoken truth. I choose to no longer live a life that keeps reflecting a painful youth, because I've discovered within myself that there are greater truths to live, therefore I can no longer allow the past to stand in the way of what I have to give.

A dirty little secret

In the summer of 1992 I left behind the only life I knew in the Virgin Islands. Though I left behind a place affectionately known as "Natures Little Secret," I left with many secrets of my own. Not the kind of secrets nature intended. Too many secrets to keep for an 11-year-old soul who had so many expectations to meet, but no one around who could see or understand the pressures at my feet. When I set foot in New York City it didn't take me long to realize that I had to go from island boy to city boy in a New York minute or else get lost in it. I arrived to an excited mother who was happy to welcome her son. I remember the drive home from the airport because it was representative of a new life I had begun. It was when I saw and felt the warmth of the New York City sun set for the first time, and when I hoped that the days and years ahead would be as kind. This was my chance I thought to live life anew, until of course new nightmares were soon to become true.

For a moment, life with my mother in Brooklyn, where we lived with her aunt, was ok. I saw a whole lot of Robert, who at the time was my mother's fiancé. Robert who my father never knew I called daddy for the first year or so, was the man who was going to complete our family with my mother and I. He was a star in the religious circles within which we lived. As well as to the church family in front of whom he had proposed. On the outside he was the Christian young man who loved my mother and accepted her son as his own. But on the inside he was pursuing a wicked agenda, and much like a wolf in sheep's clothing, he was a great pretender. Time would soon tell us that he was a joke, when the truth tripped him up and tore off his cloak. Unfortunately, this didn't happen soon enough to prevent many tears, Robert remained a dominant presence in our lives for several years.

Little did I know I'd have even greater challenges to face at school, adjusting to life within the New York City school system was its own major stressor. I wasn't prepared for the type of environment that existed within the four walls of "Weeksville Elementary School", or "J.H.S 210 Elizabeth Blackwell" which the students affectionately called "210." These were supposed to be institutions of higher education, but they felt more like the prisons many of us would end up in across the nation. It was hell everyday for me; an island boy with an accent was the last thing I wanted to be. In the islands I was accustomed to going to school in an environment that encouraged me to be the best student I could be. Then suddenly I'm in a school where for being smart there is a penalty. I do not know how any child survives this type of environment and manages to grow up to be a productive citizen of the world. It was a harsh reality out of which many didn't make it. It was easier to succumb to it than to effectively shake it.

*All the craziness that was J.H.S 210 began on "Freshman day," one of the most stressful days in my life as a child. It was the day that I learned what it meant to be a freshman, and what it meant to be on my own. I'd heard horrible rumors about what happens on this day from fellow classmates who had older siblings who had gone through it. So on that morning my typical fears and anxieties, reached new dreaded heights. I just wanted to be as small and as invisible as possible. Unfortunately, I witnessed so many students being bullied and teachers turning a blind eye to what they couldn't help but see.

Freshmen were slaves in this school, the older students,

many of whom were loaded with all kind of weapons and drugs, made us get their lunches as well as give up our own. Examples were made of those who put up resistance, and teachers simply stood by, or looked away. As I was being bullied and humiliated on one particular day, a known gang member surprisingly came to my aid. I never even thanked him because I was far too afraid. I wondered if this favor was a debt that would have to be repaid. If it was, it was one he never came to collect, I always wondered what it was in me he saw that he felt he had to protect.

I remember the moment I stood with others as we waited with fear on our faces because the ringing of the "Freshman Day" bell was only minutes away. We knew that we'd have to run, because all day that day we were reminded by the 8th graders of the beatings that were to come. As the final bell rang, freshmen ran through those doors like wild horses in every direction possible. I remember running and watching others being chased as was I. Screams, crying, and shouting reached my terrified ears, and when I got far enough to look back I saw groups of students beating up on various freshmen all over the streets. I couldn't look for too long because I was still being chased myself and I lived about four blocks away.

By the time I made it home I was hysterical, and as I rushed to get in the house my mother must have heard me because she met me in the living room. When I saw her I ran into her arms and although it wouldn't be the last time

I was forced to run home from school by a chasing thug or a following stranger, it would be the last time I ran into my mother's arms. Of all the events that happened that day, and of all the tears I had wiped away, it was the coldness I felt in my mother's embrace that shocked me the most. I was stunned by the feeling so much so that I suddenly stopped crying. I pulled away feeling like I had done something terribly wrong that I should never do again. I knew then that the only way to prevent it from happening was to never risk that kind of vulnerability with my mother again. She became like an alien to me as I became an island onto myself.

Instantly, the fantasy of the life I had hoped to have with my mother was completely over, and the lonely reality had begun setting in. I had a hard time believing that she loved me after feeling in her arms what I never wanted to feel again. I knew in my heart that we could never be a family. It would be her and Robert, and far in the background, living with a very real sense of insignificance would be me.

In the background of their lives is exactly where Robert wanted me to be. He made that clear to me one day as we waited for my mother in the car, when he said that he wished I had never been born. By the time he was bold enough to make such statements to me, he knew that he could talk his way out of anything that I would tell my mother. I knew it too. So there were many things that happened which she never knew, and some of which took place right in front her face. But it didn't matter because the truth spoken by me had no weight with her, it had no place.

I had no words to tell her, or my father for that matter, who always told me to let him know if Robert ever touched me. I was re-living the memory of the last time I was molested in Tortola several months earlier, before I moved to New York. I wanted to be with my mother and never return to the islands. I thought I would be safe from people who touch children in this way. How wrong I was to believe such a thing.

My first indication that things would go horribly wrong was when my mother, Robert, and I got a ride home from church in a car with some other church folks. The car was too crowded so I ended up sitting on Roberts lap. Apparently he was very "excited" about that. There was no way to explain to myself why my mother's boyfriend and my future stepfather was becoming aroused with his future stepson sitting on his lap. So I blamed myself and kept it inside. I didn't explain or say anything to my mother who was sitting right beside. I felt helpless like all the other times I was right where someone wanted me. Although he was a grown ass man and I was a child I can't help but think that in someway I would be blamed and he would be excused. As time passed, I buried this with all the other secrets I had been keeping. Though the events never left my consciousness, I lied to myself about whether they were real as I lived with the devastating effects of how they made me feel.

My mother finally found out that Robert wasn't the man he had made himself out to be, after it was discovered that a young lady in one of our sister churches was pregnant with his baby. With this and other related news the engagement was off and he drastically dropped out of our lives, but he didn't go quietly. He somehow managed to blame it all on me. He told people I was the reason why he and my mother didn't work out. I suppose from his point of view the fact that he was a lying piece of shit had nothing to do with it.

In any case he didn't have a positive influence on my relationship with my mother. After all it was a war between us for my mother's trust, until I no longer cared enough to fight. In the end it was his own doings that brought him down; last I heard he ended up in prison where criminals abound.

Enter Oprah

I wanted so badly to leave behind the life I knew in the islands but the funny thing was although things where so different in Brooklyn, in some of the worst ways they were the same. I still lived in the head space of the abuse I endured and re-lived every day. Although I was years removed from it, it may as well have been yesterday because I had no idea how to deal with it. I thought that somehow if I left behind the secrets I had been forced to keep, they would go away with time. What happened instead was that they became much more mine. Somewhere along the way, I stopped keeping those secrets, and they started keeping me. They were a part of my daily consciousness and they defined my identity.

When I watched The Oprah Winfrey Show for the very first time, it was as though she came through the television and into my life, illuminating the darkness with her insight. The very first episode I can recall seeing was one in which Oprah disclosed the sexual abuse she endured at the hands of her uncle and the impact it had on her life. I don't think I ever cried more than I did that day, because for the first time in my young life, I knew a name for my secrets other than my own… molestation. I was not alone. I was not to blame. There was life beyond the damage being molested had done to me. On that day my secrets lost some power over me, because of Oprah I had begun to see myself very differently. Through her words and encouragement I slowly realized that I was someone, someone special, waiting for me to discover.

Almost two decades later, as I watched Oprah announce that she would be ending The Oprah Winfrey Show after 25 years on the air, I cried like the very first day I had seen her years ago. Suddenly I was 11 years old again looking intensely at this woman who I'd never seen before and feeling like I don't know why this feels so right. But I have loved learning from Oprah Winfrey's life. She came into my life and turned on the light. She showed me what was right in front of my face: There is so much beauty in the world to be seen, if we can just get the vessel (ourselves) clean. She helped me to see what God has already given me, which is the gift of my own being. To Oprah I am so deeply grateful that I got to live the same time as you! You have exemplified not only what it means to live, but what it means to truly be anew.

A desire to speak

When I arrived at the gates of John Dewey High School, one of the best in the country at the time, I was no longer the island boy afraid of what might take place on freshman day. I had already been through the worst of what life in NYC had to offer me. I was at the right place to begin to discover me, call it timing or destiny what ever it was I loved the energy I felt at John Dewey. It was a long way from where I lived but I didn't mind the almost 2 hour commute out of the ghetto to the far more peaceful neighborhoods that surrounded this school. I had the opportunity as a freshman to join the social scene via the many clubs that were available.

After a few months there, I couldn't help but notice the school's newsletter, "The Matrix", as it made its way from students' hands to the garbage bin. I saw this as an opportunity to produce a newsletter that spoke to students in a way they would value so I created my own, "*Issues.*" Shortly thereafter "*Issues*" debuted with 750 copies versus "The Matrix's" 3000. I competed by featuring articles about relevant social issues facing students of all kinds. It was a very successful launch, but one that was met by jealousy from competing newsletters produced by more established clubs. Despite the success of the editions that followed, it was an uphill battle. One that I, as a freshman, was unable to fight in an environment where the ruling seniors thought that I was doing too much way too fast.

After a few weeks of thought and deliberation between the members of my club and I, we rebounded with a new determination and a great new idea. We were going to produce the school's first ever talk show. Named affectionately after our school, "*The Dewey Discussion Den*" was launched after a major in-school advertising campaign. We knew that if this were going to end well we needed to begin with one hell of a premier. So, I enlisted my fellow colleague and friend, John, to be the host of the program.

The day of the Premiere came, and as Executive Producer, I was busy making sure that everything was in order with the set, production schedule, and the guests. John and I stood by the door greeting members of the audience before they were seated. All I remember is becoming increasingly nervous when the audience poured into the room for the show. I was never more excited about anything else in my life as I was at that moment.

The other producers filed in and were introduced, and now it was time for the show to begin. As our theme song played and I listened to the words of "Imagine," written by John Lennon, I connected with the verse where he sings, "*You may say that I'm a dreamer, but I'm not the only one, I hope someday you'll join us, and the world may live as one.*" It was then in that moment I knew, that this is what I was born to do. Though I had denied it because of my fears of being in front of an audience, the moment of truth had arrived. The song was over and I heard the audience's applause. As we were going in, John turned to me with the microphone in his hand and said, "This belongs to you." He knew it and despite my fears, I knew it too.

Though he stepped down as the host of the program, he stepped up as my strongest supporter and my biggest fan. The show became a great success because it was a show created by the students, for the students, and because of the students with whom we connected by covering relevant issues such as child abuse, gang violence, and teen sex. We were able to provide a forum for students not only to speak but one that spoke to them in a way that showed them they were not alone.

Unfortunately, life outside of school wasn't so great. I was tired of New York City life. I was tired of the church, home, and school routine. On the surface it might have seemed that I lived a sheltered and protected life, but the only thing that was sheltered was my mother's view. She could not, or would not see the hell that was my life. But it was a reality I wasn't willing to live with anymore. I was so over it and although it would mean leaving John Dewey High School which I loved, it would also mean leaving the life I knew in New York City with my mother which by this time I had grown to hate.

Life in Killeen Texas

In the summer of 1997, I was 16 when I left New York City to live with my aunt and her two sons in Killeen Texas and enrolled in Killeen High School as a junior. Thankfully, my mother and aunt were open to the idea of allowing me to relocate. I loved just about everything in Texas, but what I loved the most was that it wasn't like New York City in any way. The first year in Killeen was the best year of my life up until then, but soon things deteriorated and before long I'd know a hell that had nothing to do with the relentless Texas heat.

My aunt Evelyn who I had only previously known from a distance, was the type of person who I always thought of as supportive and understanding. She was also the last hope I had for a functional relationship with an immediate family member at that time. While our relationship was functional, it was so only on a superficial level. Neither she nor I were prepared to deal with the issues that stood between us. She believed that she could do better with me than my mother had been able to. I suppose it's the nature of women to desire to nurture, but the fact of the matter was that she simply could not give me what she did not get. She couldn't fix me in all the ways and places I had been broken. How do you repair something when you don't even know what is broken, and the tools you're using to fix it are damaged as well. For, she too was broken like all the rest us. We are a family, like so many others, who prefers not to deal with the harshness of reality. Especially when the fantasy is more acceptable than the truth we refuse to try..

In the last six months before I returned to the Virgin Islands I had gotten the idea that my aunt no longer desired to have me in her home. I figured that she must have been disappointed with my grades, because I was barely making it academically for reasons neither she nor I could understand at the time. Whatever it was that she had concluded, she decided that some sort of counseling might help. It did not. Frankly, I felt that she could have used it much more than I at the time.

As the months went on she grew cold and distant towards me. In fact she resorted to communicating with me only through notes. I thought this was pathetic for a woman who professed that she was so much more evolved than the rest of us in the family. I overheard many conversations about me that she was having over the phone with various members of the family, including my mother and father. That seems to be somewhat of a tradition in my family.

They all have so much to say about me but never to me. Anyway, it didn't take long for aunt Evelyn to successfully convince them of what they already believed... which was, that I was out of control.

She did such a wonderful job of demonizing me that my distant absent father decided to call me and reprimand me over the phone. I allowed him to call me several more expletives than I should have, and although I wanted to hang up the phone on him, I decided that my future years of silence would speak more loudly than I could at this time. So I just gave my aunt the phone and they continued to rant and rave. I wasn't really surprised that I was experiencing all this drama because, after all, I was living with family. What did surprise me was that my aunt was capable of being so small and so low. To this day, I don't know how she justified her actions as an adult, or as my mother's sister who was trusted to take care of her son.

I found myself in a familiar place once again where nothing I had to say would matter. Just like it was when I was living with my mother in New York, and Robert had convinced her that she could believe nothing I said. When aunt Evelyn started to remove the soap from the bathroom after she and her children had showered, who was going to believe that? Who was going to believe that all of a sudden food was in short supply? And who would believe that one day when I came home from school, they would have completely moved out of the house without telling me of their plans? No bed, no chairs, no nothing, they were gone. Who would believe that I slept on the floor in a light-less empty house at least a couple days after my mother, who I was extremely angry with for much of the same reasons I was angry with my family in general, called and gave me the address to my aunt's new house.

In the face of all this madness I had some wonderful friends in Texas, who fed me and were there to support me through all of this. Some of them were even bold enough, or maybe they were just too disgusted with the way I was being treated, to not be silent when they saw my aunt. Some of them went as far as trying to take legal action. I remember talking with lawyers of one family in particular that wanted to adopt me, as old as I was. In the end we decided that since my 18th birthday was around the corner it would be best to wait. As time went on, waiting became less of an option for me because I wanted nothing to do with family, period. So I made plans to run away; never to be seen or heard from again. But God laughs when humans plan.

A few days before I had planned to disappear, I was sitting in class and like most days my thoughts were miles away. My thoughts, however, were interrupted that day when I heard God's voice for the first time. I can't tell you what this experience truly felt like; it seems that the magnificence of it is the very keeper of its secret. Nevertheless, God said to me in that moment that I had to go back to Tortola where I had spent a significant part of my childhood living with my grandparents. I firmly believed, Tortola was never an option for me, because this was where I was sexually molested and abused as a child.

My response to God was one of fear because I felt that I couldn't return to face my past there. That is when an overwhelming feeling of peace came over me, and God told me that there was a reason why I need to go back. Everything was going to be alright. For the first time I knew that I could face the future with confidence, and although, I had no idea what God's plans were for me in Tortola, I surely wanted to find out.

My friends in Texas all thought I was crazy. They pleaded with me not to go back, asking how I could return to that place when I had a choice? The only answer I could give to these extraordinary people, who had opened their lives, their hearts, and their homes to me, was that I wouldn't have to face it alone. This was the truth that empowered me in the face of my aunt's silent cruelty, the voices from the past that played in my head telling me that they wished I were dead, and the abuse against which I had measured the worth of my life. A life I now knew was bigger than all of that. My realization was that I had to go back to Tortola, a place where I had been made to feel so low, to rise up in the faces of those who treated me so.

My feelings concerning my family in general have evolved much like I have over the years. I have learned to love them, forgive them, and see them through the eyes of compassion because I have learned how to do all of that for myself. I hope each and every one of them learns how to do the same, because in that process I've come to the realization that hurting and hating is a waste of my time. This book is a look at what was, and what I now choose for there to be. Once upon a time Tortola was my ground zero and God took me back there and showed me that I could be a hero. He showed me that I mattered in the face of so many things that did not. He reminded me of who I could be just when I totally forgot.

What this journey has taught me is that no one who makes it does so alone. If I became a hero it was on the shoulders of the many heroes that I had, who taught the importance of solidarity. I remember the many days after school going home on the trains of New York City with a group of my friends, some of whom had decided they'd take the long way home, just so we could all be together as long as possible before going our separate ways. They would always say to me "Akil don't forget us when you become famous," as though they knew something or saw something in me I did not. One thing was for sure though, they believed in me more than I could ever have believed in myself at that time.

I could never forget them because they were the first to see me in a light I was unable to see myself in. Sometimes it's the light shed by others that enables us to truly see our own. This has become my mission in life: To be a light in the world that enables others to truly see their own. Because I know, once that happens, we will realize our own greatness and in doing so, we will value each other more as we learn to value ourselves. This is my hope, reflected in the upcoming collection of articles, some written over a decade ago, many published during my years as a columnist and radio talk show host; all inspired by a life of learning how to love and be loved in return.

Section One

The truth I come to bring is to tell you that you are your one true finest thing.

TITLE: *Sleeping Dogs No longer lie*
INSPIRATION: *This article was inspired by a relationship that was changing with an aunt who I yearned to please as a child. She represented the hold that people we love can have on us when we can only see ourselves through their eyes, but I woke up when I began to see my self through my own.*

My mind is made up, now it's time for the shake up. Are you ready for the wake up? For this sleeping dog is among those who no longer lie. While I have been sleeping I've been dreaming that I can fly. While asleep to the truth I've seen a new reality through God's eye. I have been under the illusion of a false ideology, and sedated with a heavy dose of inferiority. You have attempted to get me to abort a great possibility, But you will tell them that "I am smelling my piss", that comes from the inferiority list. It's how you say, "get back in your place," and it holds the connotation that I am worth no more than waste. It is really your self-image you are projecting. It distracts others from your insecurities, which you are protecting. You are more concerned with controlling others, than character perfecting. Now that I have blown up your spot, you should know I have the power to destroy any masks that you've got. So I won't ask you to release me, because it is simply not your choice. I no longer look to you to complete me, nor do I seek comfort from your voice. You say that "I am smelling my piss" and

I know for sure, that is not true, because the urine on the floor, honey, is coming from you.

Are you ready to take me on, because I'm well rested, you've made me strong. I'm ready for all you've got, so go ahead take your best shot. Your fears have been predicated and I just realized why, because you now know sleeping dogs, no longer lie. With the puzzle you have us confused, and with the muzzle you have us tamed. And, in the name of Jesus, you have us enslaved. Your methods no longer hold power, because our ideology has been reconsidered. When we woke up your influence withered. We no longer endure, the enslaving pains. It is our decision, to break those dog chains. They held us not, because of their power, it was a trick of the mind, that caused us to cower. The idealisms we had, which we now recover, have given new hope, for us to discover. So now we realize, the same way we broke free, is the secret to changing, the world in which we be. The secret is in our mentality; we stop waiting on the world to change and realize that we are the change that needs to be. No more "poor black me, the white man has taken away my identity." You are the author of your own possibility, you must reform your own ideology. After that, there will be, for you, a new reality! The life you want, you can realize it, order it up and then super size it.

TITLE: *The Relic*

INSPIRATION: *After a break from writing my weekly column in the newspaper I wanted to tell the readers that although I have felt discouraged, disconnected and dead, like so many of them. I am a relic, and within, there lies a relic in us all. We may stubble with disappointment, we may fall in shame but on the shoulders of faith we will rise again.*

I am grateful to be back talking to you again. I return with a very different point of view, after having been up-rooted, now my roots are all brand new. With new ground in which to grow, I look forward to learning things I even didn't know, I did not know. For the things I thought I had figured out, I now look over once again, and I see now there is so much more for me to comprehend. As we grow into more sophisticated skin, we realize the wisdom in rethinking everything within. As we grow, we see life from many different frames of mind, and there's nothing wrong with that, it's part of the journey towards being more refined. For life doesn't allow us to go forward unaware, the more life we experience, the better for us, and the sooner we get there.

I'm doing the most difficult work that any of us can ever do, and that is the restructuring of the inner you. The honest one-on-one with ourselves, is the hardest interview. It is our own truth, that is the most difficult to pursue. I made an investment and at the same time, I took a chance, all the while I was shaking in my pants. I'm still here today, but in a better frame of mind, and I can't begin to tell you of the new self-worth that I find. All I can tell you is, that it finally feels so good to be me, where I am with myself today, I never knew that I could be. I am grateful for my progress, but not in any way self-satisfied, for I haven't even begun to do the work which the savoir hath provide. I no longer have to ask you, excuse me while I rise, that is a question I must ask myself, that is what I now realize. I do ask your pardon, in case you do not understand, for what I am growing into, is an honorable man. You do not have to understand the path of travel which I choose. You do not even have to be enthused. I am not beyond the screw-ups. We are all entitled to that much. It is what we do there after that separates each of us. Life is poetic that's what I always say. Our mistakes are half the poetry and we make them everyday. There's nothing wrong with faltering, just make the missteps new. So you can grow to do and be, things people thought impossible for you. Our mistakes are not what decide our destiny. It is what we then do with them, that makes life like poetry.

I will not complain about what I cannot control, rather I will let the world's troubles be an inspiration to my soul. We shouldn't be discouraged, though I know we all get like that sometimes, but if we live where love is, it will renew our hopeful minds. It's hard to stay in that place, but we can live there, and be kept by God's grace. I'm going to keep on walking, to the Promised Land. Though at times the road there seems like, it's laden with quick sand. I have some wounds from the battle, some scars on my hands. You can count them one, two, and three, they are symbolic of the relic I know myself to be. Just because you screwed up, doesn't mean that it is done. It is what you do afterwards, that decides the final outcome. Just because you screwed up, doesn't mean you're dumb, it is how you rise up out of it, that displays your true wisdom. Screwed up, bruised up and used up, we clearly may have been, but within us there lies a relic who will certainly rise again.

TITLE: *What are we growing into?*

INSPIRATION: *I was inspired to write this article after reading a book by Dr. Wayne Dyer called "Change Your Thoughts Change Your Life." For me it was about becoming more of who I was meant to be and more aware of what has been growing in and out of me as I changed my thoughts to create my desired reality.*

Growing up is hard to do. Apart from that we have to be careful of what we are growing into. Still it takes a great deal of wisdom and understanding to make choices that really represent who we are. Rather than those choices, that represents who we don't want to be. We are a choice away from being, either a menace or part of the solution for our society. A choice that is up to you, and a choice that is up to me. We can be a voice, that speaks hope or hate in our community. Growing up is hard to do; yet we must be mindful of what may be growing in and out of us. With our hope in humanity fading, on the brink of insanity silently suffering, who can we share our thoughts with, and who can we ultimately trust?

Trust! Some of us don't believe in such a thing, we say no thank you to the pain trusting can bring. It's easier to carry on in the ways that we do, living, believing and speaking thee on untrue. Although we feel somehow we need an answer, we don't have the will to search for a cure for our cancer. But that is where our growth lies. It's in those issues that bring tears to our eyes. Yes growing up is hard to do, because it means becoming a better you. It is part of what we were born to do; yet we must be mindful of what we are growing into. There is always someone or something, trying to take us over, to tell us who to be, what to think, and what to say, moreover. It happens to the masses every day, in the name of Allah, Saint Mary, and the Jesus way.

Growing up is hard to do because you have to guard against what wants to grow into you. There are many lies that wish to become true, and they are just waiting to be accepted by you. There is much to become aware of, and so much more to consider. We are all pilgrims on a journey to learn, how to love and become less bitter. To learn how to forgive yet still be willing, to give what we have come to deliver. Growing up is something we should never stop doing, because our better selves are always worth pursuing. Attaining what we each have the potential to be is in turn our greatest gratitude, offered up for our creator to see. The work we love is that which is worth doing. Who we have the potential to become through our passion for that work, is well worth pursuing. Nothing else is worth your time, because time, unlike money, we can't stow away. All we have is this moment of this day. And I chose to use it, to say all I've said here today. Why? Because growing up is hard to do, let us be mindful of what we are growing up into.

TITLE: *Taking out the trash*

INSPIRATION: *God was talking to me on the day I wrote this article. He showed me a new way to look at a situation I was angry about, as He often does.*

I found myself deep in thought while I was picking up trash outside the Guard shack where I worked as a security officer one day, and I have to tell you they weren't pleasant thoughts. I was picking up trash that should have never been there in the first place. Trash that was placed there by one of the nastiest people I have ever had to work with. The trash needed to be removed, however, because it was a negative reflection on our company and us. So, while I was picking up carelessly discarded candy wrappers, soda cans and straws, I had the thought that even though we as individuals may not be responsible for producing the "trash" in our world, we are responsible for cleaning it up. Why, because we know better, and we are all responsible for what we know. Robert, my co-worker doesn't know better, though he should, and I certainly do. Surprisingly, he came to me the next day and thanked me for cleaning up for him. I thought, "for you, no Robert, for us."

By the time I finished picking up all the trash that day, I had a bag full. And as I proceeded to the dumpster to throw it out, I felt as though I was throwing out the trash in me as well; the mental trash that I had initially been thinking. It is the kind of trash, which prevents us from seeing the work that we must do. What it tells us is, "that person's problems have nothing to do with us." There's no difference between the man who pollutes the earth, and the man that allows the pollution to remain. However, he who embraces the cause of emancipation preserves the opportunity of salvation for all men who choose to not remain the same. That is the greater work, which we all must do; it is to choose each day to live anew. To find new ways to love your brother is to rise, yet still, lift up each other. After you wipe your tears, wipe those of another. Love is strong because it needs to be, and not just for the moment, but for all eternity. We need to love to preserve salvation for one another, when we take out someone else's trash we show love for our brother. Although we don't know how many chances others may need. In love we must be there, until they are ultimately freed. To be free is their choice, and although it is their fight, when we continue to love each other, we serve as a guiding light.

TITLE: *I am enough*

INSPIRATION: *The storm I speak of in this article is depression, which has taught me so much about myself. Depression forced me to confront all the painful issues and answer all the questions that I'd been avoiding all my life. I thought depression showed up in my life as a problem, but God showed me that I could make it the start of the solution instead. After I answered the enemy within me, I could care less about the private and public critiques alike. All that mattered is what I thought about myself. This article was about putting the public on notice.*

I knew that the day would come where I'd have a more intimate revelation of the wisdom held in the messages I have been so deeply inspired to share. That day my brethren has arrived with great fanfare. While my dreams have taken a beating, I've learned the lesson of hope worth repeating. And while my faith I've been left humbly seeking, I decided to cease public speaking, since holding on caused my strength to seriously weaken. I've held on in the past to many things no longer in my grasp. The storm has left me with nothing else but me. It left me empty to show me my fullness. It brought out my worst to show me my goodness. It left me weak so that I may be a witness to my own inner strength. It took me through hell so that I could experience a deeper appreciation for heaven. Yes the storm crushed my hopes so that I would learn how to keep hope alive. As I sat in the eye of this storm with nothing and everything I needed, I realized out of the blood I bled, flowed the knowledge that I am enough, I am not dead.

I lost my voice but I got it back, and as I reemerge I do so with a message that is still intact. My arms are too short to pat my self on the back, and so I'm still so far from the man that I want to be, yet I am so much more of a man than most others I see, though such comparisons mean very little to me. For who I am and whom any of us ought to be, should never be defined by another mans inadequacy. I lost myself and in the struggle to hold on to me, I gained a more introspective view of the suffering of humanity. I thought if I only knew that there would be such a time as this, where holding on to my values would become my only wish that I'd somehow be more prepared for this precipice. Now all I have left is a truth for which many line up to hear, but few among them are truly worthy of an affair so intimate and dear. Of course they believe that they all ought to be, but it is I who decides who is worthy of me. With that decision lays a personal responsibility, to share my own truth with the utmost dignity. So with confidence I say no, to both public and private scrutiny. If you really have to pry, you are not worthy, so please don't try. The knowledge you ask for, is simply not your privilege to know, this is what you've decided by the path on which you've chosen to go.

Section Two

As long as there are roads there will be bumps
in them. Don't worry about the bumps
concern yourself with your suspension.

TITLE: *The Coin*

INSPIRATION: *Growing up in New York City as a teenager was the point in time in my life when I decided to begin to embrace myself and all the qualities that made me who I was in the face of those who tried to make me something else. I'm glad I chose to be me, in light of the fact that, at times, I had hated myself. Choosing me marked the beginning of me taking responsibility for all the issues that were mine.*

Two sides of me, the side that's authentic, and the side I won't let be. The side that wishes to speak and the side that suffers silently. Two roads to walk; where I stand now there's a fork. Two questions that I must answer before I choose which way to go. Will I live a life under the influence of those I know? What will my legacy be, a tale of a man driven by insecurities or of a man that I was afraid to be? If I am to become who I truly ought to be, which of these roads is suitable for me? As I ponder these questions, and as I start learning to forgive my self for my imperfections, I reflect on the songs of yesterday which helped me to see myself in a brand new way. I am no longer the same today, because I have also learned, how to pray. I look at life now, from two different points of view, and in reflection of what I've been through, I now have learned how to balance the two.

I call it the coin. And like a coin, both sides are true. I try to walk in between the lines, because I don't like what each extreme defines. This task is very hard to do, because people won't let you be you. They have labels for your head, and to live restricted by those is to be dead, because then all you are instead is what someone else has said. Though you may try to turn me on heads or tails, rather I'll decide, my decision prevails! Some even try the use of force, to put me in groups and classes without remorse, but I'm more than a label -- please understand, I hope your able – to think beyond your years, step outside of yourself and leave behind your fears. To see whom I wish to be, and realize that a label could never define me.

The coin is no longer a mystery; I now understand its history. For me the coin of pain carries wisdom on its tail, but the coin of wisdom isn't spent much, so the coin of ignorance will often prevail. The other side of that coin is the feeling of not being accepted or understood. We have traded in our true selves long ago for wealth and fame it seems, but it only looks that way with coins of ignorance in your jeans. I'm troubled by what I see! I must forge a path because there's none for me. My only direction is from within, because I must live inside my skin. And the coin of wisdom that I now spend was reborn from the pain that has become my best friend.

There are questions that still remain: What do you have in

your hand? What are you willing to spend to understand?
What have you traded or pawned already? What have you
lost, what are you willing to gain?

If you don't understand me, hold it steady. I'm my own
voice; I'm not projecting any. I'm my own choice, not the
choice of many. My friends, I don't see any. They were with
me though, last time I checked, before I decided that it was
okay to be a reject.

TITLE: *The Red Carpet*

INSPIRATION: *When the heat of the sun became
too much to bear, God blew me a cool breeze that
revealed an inner strength of which I was not aware.
Things worked out as they always do, but we get tired
when we neglect to renew. In this article I share the
events of such a day, when I sincerely doubted that I'd
find my way.*

I wonder what life is like for the ducks in Roger Williams
Park in the heart of Cranston, RI? That was the thought
that ran through my head as I sat in my car by a lake there
last Monday at 6:24 pm a few blocks from home. I was
watching the seemingly carefree ducks after a long, hard
day at a job I knew would not work out for me. It was an

8-hour-long trial period at one of those sales jobs, where you go door-to-door trying to sell merchandise to people who aren't interested. As I trudged around the neighborhood with two other guys who I was paired with for the day, many thoughts ran through my mind: "I wonder if I have what it really takes to be successful, not necessarily at this job, but life in general." As the day went on, my train of thought left me feeling like a failure. Then I remembered that part of being successful, is figuring out what you are not good at. And with that, I started to pick myself up from a place of fear to a place of faith.

As the ducks swam by, despite the fact that I had not eaten all day, I saw them not as a symbol of food but a symbol of faith. They reminded me of the sparrow, the forgotten bird of the sky. They are not forgotten by their Creator, and now I know, nor am I. He has been good to me in ways I can't find words to explain... He remembers me even when I forget His name. He forgives me for things I haven't been able to forgive myself for yet. His grace is the perfect picture of the place where I must get.

On days like that, when I am filled with self-doubt, He used the ducks to show me what His love is all about. His favor has been beyond explanation; the life I live is not my own creation. My life is poetic indeed, not because I write it that way, but because I live it in the glow of His favor every single day.

Everywhere I go I see doors open where walls were before. I showed up at a dealership, and left in something so nice the neighbors swore. They want to know how much I pay, but they don't understand what my explanations really say. I often ask why people roll out the red carpet for me, and they say it's something special they see. I just know God has been incredibly good to me. He has inspired my fellow men to sit me in the lap of luxury. They treat me like I have goldmines somewhere, and it's all because of the love of His care. I showed up as a window shopper with no silver or green, and I left with a new definition, of what miracles truly mean.

TITLE: *How long is forever?*

INSPIRATION: *People like to use the word "forever" as a measure of their love and commitment. But like other words that are so often misused, I have found that the meaning of the word is relative to the person that is using it or abusing it. The next time someone tells you that they will be there for you "forever," ask them sincerely, "How long is forever?"*

How long is forever?
Is it as long as you can remember?
What about from January to December?
When a friend says we'll be friends forever,
is it as long as they care to remember?
How long is forever?

How long, how long is forever?
Is it from the times you held my hand
to the times when you never?
Is it after I've given my all to you, and you
show me the same ungrateful attitude
despite all I continue to do?
So tell me how long is forever,
and what does forever mean to you?

How long is forever?
Is it from the time I drive that new car off the lot,
to the time when for a new car I must plot?
There are some things it seems you have
conveniently forgotten now that I am able to afford
what I am rocking.

You said that I wouldn't be anything without you,
that's why the loan you ask for is
something that I won't do.
You wanted me to break down,
but instead I broke through.
Now I see you coming around acting as if I
wouldn't remember how you do.
Just because I have forgiven doesn't mean you can
be a part of this life that I'm now living.

How long is forever?
When will you ever make a promise
that you'll keep?
Before again this you repeat, I believe you'll do
better if you cut your tongue off before you speak.
Before the seeds you sow, that you shall also reap.

May God be with you during your harvest time,
when the people you promise forever to,
you won't be able to find.

People you abandoned in their time of need, who
helped you in the name of love.
But you hurt them in the name of greed.

How long is forever?
When my hair gets gray, my butt sags, and my
breast no longer stand up the same way?
How long is forever?
When our marriage vows say it's me and you and
not the rest, then you go and have sex, with some
uninvited houseguest.

How long is forever my friend?
I'm tired of this emotional mess that we're in.
If you can't come good then don't come at all.
Because that would be much better, than to come,
and then to fall.
I will still love you through it all, but I ask you
again my friend of fair weather, in the midst of our
Lord, how long, how long is forever?

TITLE: *I can't stay here*

INSPIRATION: *When you follow your ambition your dreams come true, but when you follow your passion you discover the dreams God dreamt for you. On the day I wrote this piece I was fed up with the mundane reality of the job I was working, which in itself felt like its own insanity. I didn't know where to go from there, or where I'd be, but I knew I wanted out, of that which was my reality.*

Maybe there will be a bridge, or maybe there will be a boat, that has within it, a paddle to help me stay afloat. If all else fails and the rough sea prevail, at least I can rely on, the life vest of hope. I just know I can't stay here any longer, and it's not because I can't cope. I know I am much stronger, than all the obstacles ahead, and I am willing to face them, or otherwise be dead.

What is the purpose of living, if our fears prevent us our all from giving? I am willing to make a swim for it, because it is worthy of such a fight. To die for my passion, is my God-given right. To swim for the chance to live, this is my chosen fight. My life was given to me to use to shine my light. I resolved here and now, to shine it with all my might. No matter, which way the tide turns, I know I will be alright.

I don't know how rough the sea is, or what I might meet out there. But I am willing to meet my maker, because I have decided I can't stay here. If I must meet death I will not meet it, while shackled by fear of dreams I failed to pursue. I prefer to meet it in flight, fueled by faith in miracles too. Miracles we doubt, God will really do, not realizing clearly, that the miracle is you. I'm going to swim until I see the border, and with enough faith I may just walk upon water. Getting our lives in proper order is not about landing on the shore. We only become who we are, on the journey from where we were before.

Section Three

*If only the wisdom of men allowed them to see
the magnitude of God whose breath they use
to deny him.*

TITLE: *Some kind of prison*

INSPIRATION: *We live in the land of the free but the irony is that we are slaves to the establishments that be. We are slaves trying to convince ourselves that we are happy, buried under a mountain of debt trying to make up for our self worth deficit.*

Some kind of prison, where the dead have not risen. Where the cries of the children go unheard. The plight of a nation, its goals deterred. The dreams of man, God's great creation, caged like a wing-clipped bird. American society is not as free, as the bald eagle appears to be.. Not free, as some grown women and men may be, still molesting the children of our society. Or are you among those who refuse to see, and still believe we're all living free.

It's some kind of prison, where our young boys are hidden. They're locked behind a false portrayal of masculinity. By those with a façade of morality. Leaving them without a sense of identity, not knowing who they are or, where within, they themselves may actually be. No sense of self, or manhood or family, it's a state of mind that's truly sad to see.

Some kind of prison, slaves to expensive living, by this our men are driven, for they know nothing about giving. Oh yes, its some kind of prison where inmates can't see themselves as they be. They believe they are free, far be it, though, from reality.

In this prison surrounding me, are my fingerprints, that's what I see. Not those of my family, on the walls that imprison me. You too ought to look around and see, who is really imprisoning thee. You may be surprised when you finally see, you intimately know the one who holds the key.

I know it's some kind of prison, where the dead believe they are risen. I have seen the walls surrounding me, and have identified the fingerprints on them belonging to no one else but the man in the mirror that I see. I have come to realize that I have the key to the door that's locked with fear and unlocked with free. My freedom is my own responsibility, as I created the prison surrounding me.

So I know about the prison, where our young boys are hidden. I know they do not realize the reality of their captivity, because they are prisoners of their own skewed mentality. They believe they're important if they wear names others can see, but name brand goods don't erase, ingrained insecurity. It's just a cover to hide what is their inner reality. Much like condoms that provide a false sense of security, for those of us who use them in our iniquity. Not knowing they can't protect us spiritually.

There are no short cuts on the road to responsibility. There's only one way to become the man that you should be. But it begins with the end of our prison mentality. It's some kind of prison... When will we be free?

TITLE: *The Unholy Ghost*

INSPIRATION: *I dedicate this article to the approximately one million people worldwide who lose the battle with depression every year and commit suicide. It is my belief that although they made the final decision, hearing the echoes of unsupportive voices made it that much easier. On the day this piece was written I sat in the security vehicle of a shopping mall parking lot in Hingham Massachusetts where I worked as a security officer. I remember it well because I won one round of what had felt like a loosing battle for so long.*

I try to look at life's challenges as opportunities to rise to a higher level of consciousness. For I believe that trouble and controversy are but questions posed to us, measuring the strength of our character and the depth of our integrity. The greatest battles we fight are those within our own hearts, and our most formidable opponent resides there also. I'm no expert on these matters, what I speak of are my own experiences and what I share are my personal thoughts. This article is very difficult for me to write because it's about an issue I have yet to overcome, the issue of depression. I believe that the kind of depression I am now experiencing is a destructive force born out of deep self-hated and raised with a profound lack of self worth. This beast feeds on everything one perceives to be wrong with themselves, and he is skilled in the area of promoting self-destructiveness. His methods of self-extinction are far more sophisticated than even those who are experiencing it seem to know.

Every day I live with it, carries the threat that he shall overcome. His weapons are very powerful. He uses my insecurities to beat me into submission and leaves me powerless to speak. He confuses my mind with distortions, making me think he will always be there. He is in control most of the time; my decisions are his, disguised as mine. The battle I fight it's all in the mind, my thoughts and his, are all intertwined. I can't find rest from this enemy, no matter where I go he finds me. He seems to be my kryptonite, the nearer he comes the more I lose my power to fight. He laughs at people with their well-intentioned advice; to know the real deal, they ought to think twice. They know not the battle, they think to die is my choice. They can't tell from my words or from the tone of my voice.

He uses my God given gifts as he pleases; he wields my sharp tongue to tell lies that keep others at bay, as the noose he squeezes. His greatest wish is to decide for me. Even better, if I surrender out of pure agony. (*This transition represents my awakening after which I realized the purpose of depression in my life.*)

I've been beaten and I've been bruised. I've been hurt, and I've been used. I may have been, but I'm no longer confused. Let the war begin. I speak to you, "The unholy ghost." The name depression, you're known by the most. I see your fingerprints all over, those you use as your host. You target family and friends, yet you escaping detection is one of your notable trends. For to fight an enemy you must know who he is. You must know what you're up against, or the battle is his.

I must admit your methods are good; you've broken me down like no other enemy could. Now as I rise with each brand new day, I have decided, on my own, I will not live your way. I began this war with many in mind; so many have died, now it's your time. I contemplated your existence, but now your purpose is clear. You come to ask me who I am, and who I fear? You challenge my answer by altering my reality. Now I realize the deeper question to actually be, how willing am I to live, and with what intensity.

I don't know if you can feel the heat, but it's been getting warmer with each word I speak. You have challenged my existence, you have made it difficult to be me, but in the process you have strengthened my desire to find my true destiny. And while I continue along this life-affirming journey, I do so, with a greater sense of hope in what is possible for me!

TITLE: *I almost let go*
INSPIRATION: *I felt my life spiraling out of control at a time when it seemed depression had gotten the best of me again. This piece tells the story of the day when the spiraling finally came to an end.*

As I prepare, I have no regrets, about taking you on a journey through a life that's as sweet as it gets. Wisdom comes at a price that is high, but I told God that's what I wanted my life to exemplify. He has kept His promise to love me through and through, even as I decided to give in to what my suicidal hands might do. He allowed me to hurt like I never hurt before, and rather than taking my pain away, He gave me the strength to endure even more. He showed me through its course, that life is not worth living, if it is disconnected from its source. God allowed me to let go, as He tightly held on. To show me what life looks like, when His love is gone.

Not strong enough to hold on, yet strongly desiring to let go, lately the walk through the valley of the shadow of death, has been the only walk that I know. I had decided before the dawn, that I would simply end it, and not walk on. Despite what my mother used to say, "Suicide leads you straight to hell." How was I going to tell?, It's no different than where I now live and dwell.

I understand why so many end the pain, they make the

trade to keep from going insane. If they felt they had a life to lose, death they certainly, wouldn't want to choose. Instead the inclination would be, to go ahead and live life carefree. But unsupportive voices scream and yell, "It's your choice, shut up and get well." It is those who continue to spout, who make it easier to trade this hell, for the one my mother spoke about.

Those voices inspire me to shout, so that the depressed know there's another way out. Their voices have merit too. When I stand and speak, it's on the collective strength of all of you.

We serve as His hands in each other's lives, God has shown. So that not one of us will have to make the difficult journey to the Promised Land alone.

I stood at the crossroads this morning, and contemplated taking a terminal route I've considered many times before. It's not that I don't want to live; it's that I don't want to just exist anymore. From the outside you can't see the pain I'm in. To my loved ones I'd say, "Don't call me just let me be," Except I know that person is not me. As I sat in the Barber's chair for what I thought would be the last cutting of my hair, what I heard wasn't my mother's voice warning of the hell I'd be trading, for the one in which I've been living. No, what I heard were the first and second verses of the 23rd psalm. *"The Lord is my shepherd; I shall not want. He maketh me to lie down in green pastures; He leadeth me beside the still waters. He restoreth my soul."* And He did just that.

Instead of leaving that Barbershop to go home to an early grave, I decided upon a new choice that I was given. It was a choice to seriously get on with the business of living. No, it wasn't about the continuation of this existence but about remaining to pursue the work that we all must do. Work that requires us to allow ourselves to be a canvas upon which the beauty of God may shine through. This is the gift depression came into my life to show me. It left me when I realized that in my life, God will always be.

The truth does indeed set us free, that's what happened this morning when God spoke the truth to me. He spoke life into my desolate soul and instead of dying, living became my goal. Even as I decided to give up everything, He decided, instead, to life I would cling. Filled with His inspiration, I underwent a spiritual reincarnation.

As I wrote the words above, I couldn't be reached by a dear friend who thought that I'd done what an earlier email I sent suggested that I might do. So he called 911, and I heard knocking on the door the minute I finished writing. Although God had paid a visit to my heart, to the Police, Paramedics and grief counselors, I looked like the mess I had become. I looked like a danger to myself, and as they took me to the ambulance, I heard the grief counselor say 'we all came out here for you'. She said in essence, "We came to see to it that you make it through." I thought, that's what my loving God showed up this morning to do. When I had decided that my life was worthless, I had no reason to walk on anymore, and I shut and locked my heart's front door. God came in through the window on the third floor, just to say one thing, "Akil it's time now to rethink everything!"

TITLE: *Love lifted me*

INSPIRATION: *Written around the time of my 27th birthday this piece was an acknowledgement of how far I have come and how much I have grown. Depression made the journey a very difficult one. It's like running the marathon of life on deep dunes of sand, and when I look back I see all the times when God walked with me and carried me held in His hand. Love lifted me, I didn't make it on my own, no one who makes it, makes it alone.*

As another birthday comes around for me, I am encouraged by the new day I see. What it represents is a new opportunity, to learn and grow into a better me. For I believe life's main purpose, is to discover the God within us. Another year means another opportunity to walk fully in my own shoes. While I'm here, I have another chance to become more centered and aware, that's what I choose. I'm walking forward out of the valley of the shadow of death, though the journey to the Promised Land seems so long, that is where I strive to be when I take my last breath. As I struggle to keep from slipping away over time, I also try to find and keep my righteous frame of mind. I am strangely grateful for my pain, because it was the necessary precursor to my hard-won personal gain. For it is pain that has shaped me into the young man I am today. And because of that pain, I know that there is more to me than what words or a picture can say.

Part of living is learning how to align ourselves with the delicate balance of life. We cannot appreciate life, unless we learn to live well with who we see in the mirror. You must be happy with yourself even if you don't have anyone with which to share your pillow. Even if you do, there is no happiness in the world that is true, if you don't first learn how to love you. This is why happiness eludes me, because for far too long I've allowed others to abuse me. Now those who have taught me the art of self-destruction so well, offer their hands to help deliver me from their very spell. To them I must say thank you, but no thanks. Because I've held on to their hands before, and I do not need their idea of help anymore.

I look forward to the sunrise ahead, and to God's blessed kisses, on my forehead. These days I only see one set of footprints in the sand, and I know they are not mine, yet I move forward through this trying time. As I proceed into the garden of God's eyes, I ask Him, "Where do I go from here?" Although He neglected to say, He did reply, "Let's have a conversation every day." He knows that I've lost my way, and despite what people say about the day I really tried, it wasn't medication that brought me back from the brink of suicide. No, when I looked back over God's shoulders I didn't see a trail of "feel better" pills in the sand. What I saw and felt that day, was the strength of God's mighty hand. All we need is love, that's what our hearts hurt to tell us. We are not immune from love and we shall never be. Because love is what has made us who we are, and it is what will set us free.

Section Four

I want to live with my heart opened wide enough so that others can look in and know that yes miracles are possible.

TITLE: *The road of responsibility*

INSPIRATION: *I wrote this piece when I was still a teenager, and I'm glad that I had the sense of mind to begin the journey of understanding, to help myself and others save ourselves some time.*

On the road of responsibility there are choices we have to make. We must choose carefully our company, for they may determine our fate. On the road of responsibility there will be many things to distract, but on this road you must choose to go forward never turning back. With the goal of a broken soul meeting its creator, let us be a piece of clay, in the hands of the heavenly potter who will show us the way.

On the road of responsibility there will be many exit routes, for those who get distracted and in turn deny their truths. On the road of responsibility you won't find many friends, because they took the last exit, unaware of where it ends. Many choose other paths, remaining ignorant is their choice. They will never arrive at the final rest stop, where they could relax and rejoice. On the road of responsibility it is your duty to exemplify the wisdom you have gained. Unfortunately, many choose not to be responsible, allowing ignorance to remain. They think what they don't know cannot hurt them, a logic that is nothing short of insane.

I choose to be responsible, a hard choice I do realize. I believe where there are responsibilities there should be no compromise. On the road of responsibility, I can no longer seek refuge in so-called friends, because I know the danger there, as well as where it surely ends. Many choose the reckless way on the road of compromise, the path of irresponsibility, one that's broad in its size. Ignorant people talk trash, along with their reckless choices, but may the wise be responsible, in the way they use their voices. With each choice we fulfill our destiny, and I choose to fulfill mine on the road of responsibility.

TITLE: *A child of the house*

INSPIRATION: *On Friday June 9th 2000, I had the privilege of witnessing the political leaders of the Virgin Islands debate a few controversial issues facing the country at the time. As I operated the cameras as a cameraman for "VITV," the only television station at the time, I witnessed the unfolding of a drama that would be highly publicized in the local media for weeks. I was moved enough to write the following letter (revised from the original) which I sent to all nine of the district representatives. I would have loved to be a fly on the wall as each of them opened and read this letter. [Please note that when a Virgin Islands representative is addressing his or her colleague in the congressional hall, they refer to it as "The Honorable House."]*

Hi, I'm Akil Johnson and I am writing you this letter

because I am concerned about the future of my brothers
and sisters, their fathers and mothers, aunts and uncles,
their friends and their lovers. It is with a heavy heart that I
bring this to you today. So I ask you as you read it to allow
it to have its way. Not to harden your heart, but to open it
today. Some of us have jobs where having a heart doesn't
pay, but I believe if we ought to go forward we need to help
our fellow man on his way. No thing shall prosper unless
we unite in it today.

I am concerned because our children are dying, while
we waste time in Legco, (Nickname for "The Honorable
House") crack and cocaine they're out there buying. We
don't have time to sit around and talk, about who is or
isn't lying. While we sit around and talk about it, parents
somewhere are in their closets crying, because the death
they died they now see their children dying. You may say
it's not your problem, better yet it may be, so you act, but
when you sit in the honorable house and you dishonor that
fact, it's as though you're saying that the needs of the people
have, on the laws, no impact. Instead of focusing on the
laws you focus on each other's flaws. What honor is there
anymore, in "The Honorable House" where order has gone
out the door? Can any of you answer that, without talking
fiction instead of fact?

Occupying a seat in "The Honorable house" is no different
than that of a single mother who takes care of her children

and home without her spouse. No different from a grandmother's seat, from which she feeds her grandchildren "Cream of Wheat;" children from which her own, walked away and left home. I'm concerned because you don't see, that in this "Honorable House" you are of a larger family. Instead of taking care of you alone, you should be taking care of an even larger home. We as the children will continue to die inside, which unfortunately has been the norm from which you cannot hide. What motion is more important than that, which saves this home and is not based on some trivial spat? I motion, that we all drive home the one notion, which saves the greatest portion; that says, Enough! to all the extortion, and to all the other vices that defile this home that's priceless.

As I look up at the pictures on the wall in the honorable house, I observe a sea of people however honorable they may be, who entered the world the same way as the rest of the family. I wonder if you think of it that way, because way back in that day, it didn't matter as your mothers lay, side-by-side pushing to bring you this way. They weren't talking politics that day, but about how they would raise you to pray, and to stand up for what you believe in as well as to treat your fellow man the right way.

As a child of this "Honorable House" I am looking at you all today, not as members from different parties but as members of the family in this "Honorable House." So stop a while, and take a look, because the gooses of my brothers and sisters are being cooked. And you, who hold a position in an honorable seat, are no different from that mother who has wounded children to help heal and treat. Yes our children need you to feed them some "legislative Cream of Wheat." We have wounds that we need you, in your position of honor, to help heal and treat. And if you neglect to do your duty, you are no different than the prodigal fathers and mothers whose children are left with their grandmothers. No different, in your honorable seat, for what you have neglected to do, is protect us from the very likes of you. Don't defile your honorable seat, by neglecting the children who have societal diseases to beat.

TITLE: *Call me a man*

INSPIRATION: *This piece was a message to the grown-ups in my life from my teenage self on the subject of manhood. Frankly, I was often annoyed with some of my aunts who accused me of thinking that I was a man before my time. I wanted to tell them and others in no uncertain terms that I know what it takes to be a man, what I wasn't absolutely certain of, is whether they could understand.*

Call me a man, when I can take care of a home, but not before that, you might make me think that I'm grown. Call me a boy instead, because at times I still wet my bed. And if you should see me cry, don't tell me "boy wipe your eye." Let me be a man, because tears, they understand. Don't tell me that I'm a man, when responsibility I don't take by the hand. And when it comes to doing my chores, they still end up being yours.

So how then could I be a man, when I don't know what it takes to make a stand? To be a man I must first shed the trappings of boyhood, but because I dress-up good, some think I have set foot into manhood.

The looks that you perceived - me wearing shirts that are long-sleeved - if that makes you think that I'm a man, then my friend, you have been deceived. Being a man has nothing to do with looks, casting lines, or fishing hooks. It's not about an aging thing, or how many babies, into the world, you can bring. When the truth is, you have yet to feel the sting, that making irresponsible decisions will often bring.

Being a man is about knowing how to stride, with dignity and with pride. Not so much being wild, or wearing the latest style. When even your own kids, don't know who their father is.

Call me a man, when I can stand, even in my defeat. When the very standards I claim to hold, I no longer fail to meet.

And if somebody asks you why that's the way I feel, tell them, "He's a boy – a man to be, for real."

Call me a man, when I am living out my dreams. When I am running on, determined to finish clean, not deterred by a foolish scene. When I have controlled my rage, and I can live in peace, until my final stage.

It takes more than time to become a man, that's what a boy must understand. Some never do succeed, too busy, from the vision of a man, being freed. Astray is where they eventually go. They end up nothing more than a gigolo. Along with someone's unfortunate daughter, dragging her too, to the slaughter.

It takes a real woman to know a real man, that's what women must understand. The seeds you've sown, become your life's trees, when they have grown. So don't blame others, for whom you choose, for it is you who will most certainly lose. Don't blame one-night stands on getting boozed, for letting loose and being bruised. The price to pay is high, for yesterday's choices. There are no discounts, for ignoring reasonable voices.

Call me a man, when I can stand to be alone, where I can get to know my God and walk the path that He has shown. Call me a man, when I know the Master's hand, but not before that, because then I'll know, you just don't understand… what it takes to be a man.

Section Five

It would be a shame to go through this life not ever knowing ourselves unafraid.

TITLE: *Evil Friend*

INSPIRATION: *I struggled with trusting people after being molested various times throughout my childhood. I couldn't stop myself from jumping when someone would touch me. I would apologize for reacting to their affection in a defensive way, but what they did not know was that in my mind, it was as though I had been molested yesterday. I eventually learned that the issue wasn't about trusting people, but learning to trust myself to make correct judgments about who I allowed into my life.*

What are you to me? What is that doubt that I see? It ultimately leads me to wonder, if you really are, who you say you be. Why am I not feeling free? Although love is present, trust is dilatory. So I asked God, "What is there that's left to find. What word or deed got past my mind?" I continued and I said, "Show me whether this person, is a foe or a friend." Then the answer came to me, it was something I didn't want to see. I was afraid of what the truth would be. So I denied what I knew to be the truth. I forgave, in the name of youth. Now I know, it's not the truth we must apologize for, but the signs of it, we continue to ignore.

Now it dawns on me, what kind of evil could this be? What kind of foe, is this person I do not know? One who wishes to hurt me so deliberately, after I've loved them unconditionally. All in the hope, that God would be pleased with me. Now in return, for my love I get burned. Difficult moments like these, bring to mind the injustice caused by liars and thieves. I relive how it feels after an evil touch. The loss of innocence, replaced by painful knowledge, that hurts so much. It is a reality I now comprehend, and the truth is, I've mistaken a foe for a friend.

Now changed forever, after being touched by evil, I can hardly keep it together. Feeling used, damaged, and bruised, wonder I must, about justice in the world for every boy and girl like me, who has been deceived out of their trust. We were told and we believed, that we were loved very much. Then evil changed us, with a wicked touch. Has it happened again? Has evil, come in the form of a friend?

TITLE: *Panty Sweat*

INSPIRATION: *This is the conversation that parents need to be having with their children. What will our excuses be for the misinformation that we have allowed to continue because we say we know not the proper venue? The proper time is today to educate your selves so that you can help keep your children from going astray. There are too many situations like the one discussed below, but we have to ask for the answers, even the ones we are afraid to know.*

Dear Akil,

I'm writing you this letter because I think you may be able to give me some useful advice about my situation. I'm a young lady in my early 20s, the only one among my group of friends who hasn't had sex yet. If it was up to my father I would die a virgin. I do have a boyfriend though and at 26 yrs old he has had his share, and a son to prove it. I've been with him for about 3 months now, and although he hasn't really pressured me into doing anything, I wonder how long before sex becomes the central topic of our conversations. I guess the question is if keeping him means giving it up, will I do it? I wish I could say I know what the answer to that question is, but I don't. I noticed a change in some of my friends after they finally did do it. I can't pinpoint what exactly, but it seems like they lost something, I mean other than their virginity. Now it's like they have gone boy crazy and I don't want that to be me. Why does it seem like your self-respect goes with your virginity? Akil if I were your sister what would you tell me?

Dear Sis,

I think you are already doing what is right. I would say to you now, just don't give up the fight. A cousin of mine once told me, if the relationship is right today, it will be right tomorrow, you'll see. Sex is not security, if your man wants to go, you can't hold him down with a baby. There are so many examples lately, too many brothers are shady. If you were my sister, I might want you to die a virgin too.

I wouldn't want you with a man, who only wants sex from you.

What is his baby momma's story? Don't be like the other young lady. Now I don't know your boyfriend, but the trend tends to be the same. A history, if unaddressed, can only repeat its name. Think about the real reason you are in this relationship. Is it how he makes you feel? Our friends often give up their virginity, for social appeal. They couldn't tell the difference, between what was false and what is real. I know at this age you are told by society, that this is who you have to be.

You may be a young lady, with boyfriend wanting to pop the cherry. But you have to start to think about who you want to marry. You see those other girls with one and two children already, and you say to yourself, "I don't want that to be me." Your quest for love shouldn't leave you barefoot with a baby. Your girlfriends thought that, maybe.

Bed rocking with ex-girlfriend plus child-mother knocking. Is this the life you really want to live? I'd find that shocking. Some women bend over willingly because they think that's all the love men have to give, so their boots are knocking. Meanwhile, that's all the love they can get, because from the first look their underwear has already fallen off, from panty sweat. They wake up three to four children later, because they mistook love for the alligator. You got to love yourself more than an alligator ride. Otherwise you will end up with a man, who only that he can provide.

The question for you now is, will you rewrite your

future history? Will you rise out of the cycle in which so many around you live? Or will you live the same way that is the mystery. Will you let some old notions go, to see a new vision through which your life can grow? Once you are done with that, those who don't fit in the new picture won't be coming back. They'll say, "She there pun some vibes" but that only means they don't understand what you now realize.

Dear Sister, it looks like your future is bright, but it won't stay that way, if you don't see the light. Don't give up on doing what you know to be right, and if it means you must walk alone for now, then tie your shoelaces tight. This journey is for those who stay faithful to their visions. Not to those, who allow wet dreams to make their decisions.

TITLE: *A rolling stone*

INSPIRATION: *My beloved grandmother used to call me a rolling stone for good reason. While thinking about that one day, I wrote the following piece to say to other rolling stones like myself, "It is your time, it is your season, and if you don't believe in yourself, well… here's a reason."*

I've been having a conversation with God, about being a rolling stone. I've always been referred to as one, and in my mind it has always been a sort of negative thing; but to my fellow Rolling Stones I have good news to bring. Rolling stones gather no moss; you've all heard it before. Today I will redefine this phrase to mean something much much more.

I first earned this title because of my unwillingness to settle for anything that I felt was not favorable for me. Whether that was a job, a car, or even a relationship that needed to end. Sometimes that relationship was a societal one with which I could no longer contend. In any case settling and I, have never been good friends.

My life has not been a fairy tale and at times, negative circumstances did prevail. And though it has not always been by choice, being a rolling stone has helped me to find my voice.

I was born out of troubled waters, where I lived and was raised on measly quarters. Don't mistake what I'm saying for complaining because troubled waters have always been sustaining. I've seen the other side and I have nothing to hide. I don't wish for greener grass. I am a Rolling Stone and I am not ashamed of growing up in the working class.

I've kept rolling through the pain I've endured. I was put out to pasture and completely ignored. Where all that rained on me, came from a cow's behind. But to wallow in the mire I was not so inclined. Stand my fellow rolling stones; take a bow, because, I say to you, your time is now. Rise from the manure that symbolizes your past, for that day is over and the good times are here at last.

Today I bid you, roll with courage and don't settle for the flaws. Believe that you can make a change, do not settle for unjust laws. Today I bid you, go out and burn your torches through the streets. Don't stop your marches 'til your missions are complete. Today I bid you, roll with pain, for this is from where wisdom you will gain. And if it means a lonely road you must walk, then do so until thy kingdom comes and with Him you can talk.

A Stone not rolling, is one that has accepted its own defeat. One whose purpose, is not yet nearly complete. One that has gathered no moss is one that has been faithful to the vision and today my fellow Rolling Stones that is my decision. My hourglass has no moss my friends, and if you look closely you will see that our time is quickly coming to an end.

A Rolling Stone is a beautiful element of time and as the journey is completed, it becomes something more refined. A symbol of preeminence and what we shall all aim to be. An icon and a leader, for our society. I roll on as a Stone because I aim to be a Cornerstone one day. And I will stop to gather no moss, on my hourglass display.

I'm proud to be a Rolling Stone and although I have no home to call my own, I do in my Father's hand, as a powerful instrument for my Father's plan. Rejoice my fellow

Rolling Stones, for long after you cease to be, you will be a Cornerstone for our society.

TITLE: *The emancipation of Kilo*

INSPIRATION: *I wrote this piece around my 26th birthday, it was a time when I was giving birth to a new vision of myself. Shedding the old to embrace the new, which is what growth inspires us to do. Kilo is a nickname my grandmother gave me that I have since then come to own. Like the new vision I have discovered for myself, within this freedom zone.*

How many lives is it possible to live in twenty-six years? Logically speaking a young man of twenty-six years is just getting comfortable with being grown. However, most young people are busy being products of their environments, growing themselves into who they believe they should be according to society's requirements. I have come to the realization that I am not society's creation. I am far more than my physical manifestation. More than where I live. More than what I drive. And so much more, than the thought that I've arrived.

I live in the twenty-six year-old body of an African American male. One that, according to statistics, is likely to end up in jail. That is, if I'm lucky enough, not to be shot down in the streets. Or I don't find myself, for some other reason being covered by white sheets. Too many of us define ourselves by the platinum caps around our teeth or by the corporate insignia emblazoned on what we wear around our feet. We tell ourselves what we wear is a reflection, of our success as well as our personal definition. But if we adopt that as our own, we are worth no more than our car or our latest cell phone. We'll be waiting to depreciate and expire, long before age Sixty-five when some of us can retire. We'll live and die without ever really livin', never realizing the gift of our own lives which we've been given.

Our limitations are exactly what we think they ought to be, but the question is through whose eyes do we define our identity? I need no one to cosign below, on the emancipation of Kilo. I need no one to validate me, or determine the value of my currency. We live in a world that tells us to conform for fear of being offensive, but the more I learn about who I am, the more I rise above the mental fences. They ask us to quite our voices, and to not make controversial choices. What they really want is for us to die, and for us to view ourselves through their biased eye. For this we'll be invited into the mainstream where the other bodies float, with all the others who promised never to rock the boat. But if the boat is rocked by me, someone might come to see a new vision of who they were meant to be. It may cause that person to discover a self which they did not know, because of the emancipation of Kilo.

Consider the boat rocked, and those in the mainstream, consider yourselves shocked. A massive force is about to come upon the water. The transformation promises to bring bad weather to disrupt the order. So let it thunder and let it rain, because when the storm is over you'll never be the same. A disturbance in the social atmosphere is about to take place right here. It's time to embark upon the journey of rethinking everything you know, the first step is to rethink yourself before you go.

This is the emancipation proclamation of Kilo...

TITLE: *To be known as me*

INSPIRATION: *We live in a society where people believe that it is vital to have a title. They think it somehow bolsters their identity. What I'm saying here is that I'm grown enough now to be known as me.*

The emancipation of Kilo was just the beginning, the first chapter, the first inning. In a note to myself about this life I'm living, I said no one will get in the way of what I'm healing. No one will use my past to silence my speaking. No one will close the curtains on what I'm revealing. And if it be your task to define me by a label. You should know that I've grown far past the attachment of my navel.

I'm grown enough to be known now, too rich for you to own now. I'm telling you that you can go now, because I'm enough to be alone now. I do mean now and not later, I've wasted enough time being a hater. I thought I hated you but it was me, what I hated was my false identity. It would sadden me to see one more day wasted, on that false reality I formerly tasted. Now it is the truth that I know and so it is away that you must go. I don't want to know that person that I was anymore, because I was an opinion addicted whore. What I'm feeling now, brings tears to my eyes. I didn't know pain could make one so wise. Through my tears I see someone never acknowledged, someone of whose existence I had no prior knowledge.

Now that I've found him it is my mission to set him free. The more layers I peel back the more I see, that he is truly me. Loving him the way I do, is something I never knew could be true. In a note to myself today, I told him that no one will ever get in his way. The way that I am feeling, I know within my heart is worth revealing. I must give him a chance to fully be, for he is who I gave birth to twenty six years after my mother gave birth to me. His birthday was just a few days ago. And him, I look forward to getting to know. He's someone who can't be defined by ethnicity, gender, social status or sexuality. Labels are for those who haven't yet evolved, into what they were meant to be. Those who are unaware, of the meaning of authenticity.

In a note to myself I declared myself free of the judgments of society. Indeed I am totally free from whom they told me that I could be. The real "Shorty" has shown up now, so you can hang the phone up now. For your opinion is no longer my concern. That's something I hope one day you will learn. Your assumptions no longer hold weight, to you I can still relate. But you can't tell me who I ought to be, when you don't know you and you certainly don't know me. It's alright if you must go, because you don't understand what I now know. Our relationship must end for you to see, that I'm grown enough now to be known as me.

Section Six

If faith the size of a mustard seed can move mountains, I wonder what faith the size of a mountain can move.

TITLE: *One true finest thing*

INSPIRATION: *This piece is one of my favorites, because it represents the message that is at the core of this book. It is a message of love and truth, which we must find and connect with, within ourselves.*

Through this life we are livin', we have already received the one true finest thing that God has ever given. Although it is something intrinsic we all possess, we can go through life and not realize it, never-the-less. We try to find it in other people and other things but such pursuits only sadness brings. None of these can measure up, to the value of, the one true finest thing that's already in our cup.

Since we are not aware of our own gold mine, we cheapen ourselves with the material things for which we pine. We think they make us worthy of our place, whether that be within our family, our circle of friends, or within the entire human race.

We were worthy before we were even here, for within us lives Gods breath which we should hold so dear. The value that we already have, is superior to any material salve. There are no gifts from Victoria Secret, or Mercedes Benz that are comparable to your value my friends. There are no hugs and no kisses, no Valentines Day wishes, that can replace the presence you hold that is worth all the world's gold. Your value cannot be determined by another human soul, who bases their own self worth on the size of their payroll. Your life dreams are yours to make come true, to see the truth in this you must see the truth in you.

The gift I come to bring, is to show you that you are your one true finest thing. I can take you to the mountaintop, so that you may see more clearly the essence of what you've got. Show you the beauty of the skies, but that will never compare to the beauty in your eyes. We can dive for miles just to lie on the ocean floor, but no matter what we find down there you will still be valued more. We can go to the most expensive restaurants and eat the finest cuisine, none of which would measure up to your worth as a human being.

We can buy tickets now to fly to the moon, but your beauty is more fascinating than a flower in full bloom. I'm here to tell you that the beauty of the flowers in spring, don't hold a candle to you... Your one true finest thing.

As intense as the sun in the summer time, our ability to love will always far outshine.

Fall brings with it the color of golden leaves, but nothing is more golden than the impression that you leave.

Some dread the dead of winter and the weight of the crushing snow, but old man winter is no match for the inner strength that you should know.

So it is you, you are the most special thing, and all the beauty in the world is there to honor the beauty that you bring. We come as kings and queens, but lay down our invaluable royalty to become counterfeit beings. If no one ever told you, or thought this truth to bring, always remember this my friends, you are and always will be, your one true finest thing.

TITLE: *Back Stage Pass*

INSPIRATION: *I've often imagined myself back stage at all the great things I want to do in my life. Like having my own talk show, or being a rock star, or a great thought leader. In each case I would also envision having the opportunity to speak to someone much like my younger self. My hope has always been, that I'd give them advice that would last, so without further ado here's your back stage pass.*

I'm back stage right now with only minutes to spare, and I've asked the crew members to leave, the ones in charge of makeup and hair. I wanted a minute alone before I step out of my comfort zone. For I'm about to perform on the stage of possibility, and with me walks a new energy. God has lifted me to a new place in time, now it's my responsibility to shape that destiny of mine. I speak of one vision with many dreams, and I bring one message with many themes. Think of this, as a Master Class, because you now have All Access with your back stage pass. Take a walk with me and lets go on down, I will introduce you to the many possibilities which surround.

You have to dress for the success you expect to meet, but no matter how good you look, the wrong attitude will make your wardrobe incomplete. I've lost 20 pounds just watching what I eat. I stopped taking in the negative connotations, people try to feed me through their so-called constructive conversations. I have them on the tick tock, and when their time is up, their boats will forever dock. They try to make you feel bad about your decision, but they will never win, if you make consistency your religion.

They'll come at you saying don't burn your bridges or climb upon crumbling ridges. But if the bridge is missing its support or suspension, then you are right to look at it with great apprehension. I bid you turn your back and light that match, make sure no strings attach. Then sing "burn baby burn" and be on your way, burn yourself a new path to a much brighter day.

People will try to hold you back and prevent your flowers' bloom. They'll try to frighten you with stories of certain doom and gloom. Listen, you must, and hold your head high. When you realize who you are, none of them can stop you, even if they try. When you stand in your rightful place, nothing can stifle you not even your race. When you stand up for yourself, most will back down. Those who are left standing, are the ignorantly profound. They still believe they can tell you who you should be. Don't listen to them, but repeat after me: "You are excused in your idiocy." Nobody can know better than you, who you be. Stop allowing people to dictate your itinerary. Watch those who say, they got your back, because from behind is where, cowards attack. They're playing my theme song that's my cue, I really got to run along now, but remember dreams do come true!

As I walk out the crowd goes wild, (stay with me here, I'm still in the dream sequence my child) and I begin the show this way, "**If your truth could speak to you here's what it might say:** *I have no time for those who question my worth. They wish to minimize my importance and deny my birth. They cringe when they see me moving for I am a rolling stone. They protest my movement for fear of their glass homes.*

Since life does not allow us to go forward unaware, if I haven't stepped on your door-step yet soon I will be there. Don't bother trying to get your house in order, for I come to break it down. You have been living in a glass house sitting on the sand. It's time

you move towards higher land and live on solid
ground. You have built a mansion on an ideology
that has done you no good. You can be ready when
I get there, or ignore my warnings if you think
you should. Life is poetic that's what I always say,
because I am your truth and I am under way." Lets
get this show started! Right after these messages...
(Fade to Black)

~~~~~~

TITLE: *Self Titled*

INSPIRATION: *After years of writing in the
newspaper and websites just the same, I wanted to
encourage my youngest readers to live so that they can be
proud of their name. So that, it brings them no shame, to
be known by their own name.*

There comes a time when we must stand up and own up
to who we are, then step out into the possibility of who
we can be. Our possibility is first for our own eyes to see.
Our power is first for our own selves to feel. We must know
first our own excellence before it we can reveal. When we
then know it well, the letters of our names will its glory
spell. The chapters of our lives will its story tell. Nothing

speaks louder then the lives we live, or the service that we give. That's what spells our name, and is the basis for our true fame. It steps out and tells the world who we are. Not the value of our real-estate, or the emblems on our cars.

Why get angry when people who don't know you scandalize your name? For the very "truth" they tell, they are unable to explain? Gossipmongers are like leeches, they suck your blood with their speeches. They want to bring you down with their stink, because they see your strength. They seek power by controlling what others think, and to accomplish this, they will go to any length. In their attempt to gain power they distract you from yours, if you get caught up with what is happening behind other peoples' doors. The reality that cannot be ignored, is what you think is the only thought worthy of being explored.

If you want to continue to walk like a cripple, then keep on sucking from the devil's nipple. Keep on telling yourself that you can't do this and you can't do that. Keep on complaining about what you do not have, and whose fault it is that you don't have that. Keep on running from your responsibility. Keep on blaming people for everything that is wrong with the world that you see. Breast milk is best I do agree, but it depends on whose breast you're feeding from, you must look and see. The wrong milk will make you succumb, or at the very least, it will make you dumb.

Breast milk is my metaphor for that weed you are smoking.

You know it's not just weed, right? It's laced with something that got you choking. So you know you are what you eat, right? Even if you do so, when you are out of sight. If you fart and it clears the room, you might need a check up soon. Fart is my metaphor for the ignorant things you say, which make others question your intelligence every hour of the day. The nonsense you espouse as a part of your philosophy, is not even yours, but what you have adopted it to be. Don't believe people who tell you, that you cannot change. For change is simply a thought away.

So, lets make this the day where being self-titled is not such a bad thing. When people speak your name, let them have positive truths to bring. Even if they choose to speak ugly of you, let that be anything but true. When you get in the way of what you where born to do, remember the only person who stands in your way is you.

Hopefully, you write your book, after you've grown into your better self and start to like the way you look. You won't need a title to explain what you have been through, for by the time you make it over, just your name will do. After all it is your life and it speaks for you.

My columns have gone through so many names over the years, I started out telling you that I was "Not Jus Another Voice", and although that is still true I don't need to have it in the title to explain that uniqueness is my choice. "Young Scholar" was the second act, I said then that I was on the attack. Assaulting ideas and idealisms, and while that's still true, I've broadened my objective and my message to you. Life is poetic, that's what I wanted you to know. And so I named my column that, just to tell you so.

I have a website now (ApoeticLife.com) which better defines what "A Poetic Life" means with all of it's quirks. So after all the names, mine is still spelled the same. It humbly speaks of a young man, who through words has reached out a helping hand. He wants to help his community, because he was inspired by love and a yearning to be free. The reason why I do this work I do, is so you know you are loved and anything is possible for you. Most of all my purpose is, to help you find your own, because without it you cannot find your passion, which to you should feel, like home. So now you know my brethren, that which is my aim, I now choose to do just by my name.

Section Seven

Every step you take in pursuit of someone that does not love you is a hateful act you commit against yourself.

TITLE: *They don't know*

INSPIRATION: *On the day I wrote this piece I was at work scanning files as a data entry clerk for a trust company in the Virgin Islands. I was thinking about how many of my coworkers thought they had me figured out, based on their superficial ideas which reflected on them more than me. As I have learned, we cannot live in the eyes of those who can not see.*

They don't know what I have inside
They judge me by my pride and joy
They do not know my truth
They call me ignorant because of my youth

They don't know the cards that life has dealt me
Nor the people and experiences that have shaped me
All they see is that I'm small in size
They think me weak because they see water in my eyes

They don't know where my strength or my secret lies
And when they hear me speak, their eyes open with surprise
So they scratch their heads and try to synthesize
How this young boy could be so wise

They don't know my conviction
My truth or my revelation
Nor the reason my spirit thrives
All because of blinded eyes

They don't know how to rise
When it comes to spiritual truth they're like dead flies
In the meantime though they're just telling lies
About a truth they can never realize

The more they talk the more I'll rise
And while they're busy checking my shoe size
To see if I measure up to what they fantasize
My Father will expose them in the end as spies

They will never understand my plans or my missions
For it's still being told to me in visions
I am my Father's own
And He tells me soon I'll be coming home but not alone

This journey He says isn't over yet
Let others talk, let others fret
For life is but a few short breaths
And they will be blindsided by the timing of their deaths

I know He has a plan for me
And as the days go by I understand the purpose of my ministry
That is to help all God's children see
How great they were meant to be

He wants us all to know what it feels like to be free
To be fulfilled and find your own destiny
To live your life and prioritize
To be wise and the apple of God's eyes

The journey to becoming a man
Entails much of what most don't understand
Some are comfortable with being lost
If only they knew what that truly costs

In time they will understand
In time God will fulfill His plan
And what we all must understand
Our only hope, is to hold His hand

TITLE: *Tell the children*

INSPIRATION: *As children we have to deal with the effects of what we are exposed to within the environments we grow up in. When this piece was written over a decade ago, this was a truth I was fully coming to know.*

Oh how He loves us, we are the apple of His eye. To us His love is undisguised. Saddened by those of us who do not realize that His breath is the reason we can still open our eyes. He loves us, but we think He's telling us lies. When a prophet comes and tells the truth, we send them away and we threaten to shoot; bullets of hate bullets of rage, like some of you might like to shoot through this page. There's not much you can do, not much you can say. For the workers of God will stand anyway. It will profit you not, to curse your brother, for cursing him is like cursing your mother.

Our Father says to us: Children, children can't you see, fighting your siblings is like fighting Me. Instead I want you to realize, that what you hate are the Devil's lies. If My love truly lives in you, forgive those who have done wrong to you. Let Me be the love you exercise. Unlike the one you slip in bed to surprise. My love is better than your sex. For some that might cause you to vex. No more love between the sheets, no more sex on the streets.

Christians, stop taking God places He doesn't want to go. Like down to the whore house, for He didn't make you to be a ho. Men, when are you going to realize it's not all about size. And thinking that you're better, because you're bigger than other guys. Women, there are more important things in which to invest, than the curve of your rear end or the size of your chest. We try to say outward appearances don't really matter, but watch us running constantly, to make our stomachs flatter.

How much longer before you tell your momma, that your appetite is not why you're growing broader? Fear of what she might say, "Just because I had you at 18, doesn't make it ok." Examples, examples are what children seek. What they hear is what they speak. In public, what they do, is what they see when they watch you. Our children are mirror images of us. They display the things we try to hide, from those who we secretly cuss. I say let them go, let them show the public things about us they don't know. Then maybe we shall see the error of our ways. No longer will we say Amen, nor give that fake praise.

These are the days, when behind closed doors, the hell we raise no longer stays. The children will show the world who we truly are. They are a reflection of our hidden emotional wounds, and scars. They will be just like me, telling the business of their family. They may not articulate it quite like I, but when they do, it will be so powerful that you can't deny. When the walls fall down, the demons will be looking for new fertile ground. Those children whom we have reared, reflect our emotional pain and the things we feared; it is in their hearts those demons will look to go, so tell the children, warn them, so that they will know.

TITLE: *A treasure within*

INSPIRATION: *Within us all, is the change that needs to be. Before we take the fall, we must look deep inside to see. If you're like most people tend to be, it's been buried underneath your false identity.*

I beg to differ with the unbelievers for I believe in God's treasure, and I dream of a better day where we love one another. I see a treasure in a time where the ruler is pleasure; a time where we forsake one another. Oh God be our father, for they don't know how to love us. Be our friend when our lovers forsake us. Oh God bless our mothers, the ones who still love us; help those who have left us on the doorsteps of our grandmothers. God be with the fosters; they feel like they don't have any real home. Their hope is to be at peace: they want the pain of loneliness to cease.

Expose our secrets, our treasures, and our regrets, hidden in the deepest, darkest, places of our hearts. Then no more shall we fret, no more shall we bet. Because now we can experience freedom without regret. Oh what a day, when we can play, and not feel ashamed. Even when named, our hearts still beat the same. Oh God we wonder why in spite of our leisure, which are the things in which we take pleasure. You still see in us a worthy treasure. Yes God, we wonder why You never tire, of fixing broken wings, hearts and souls that have lost their fire.

Now You have shown us a treasure, much greater than our sexual pleasure. It's Your love that holds us in an unconditional embrace. Your love overshadows our mess, our incest, and even when we are at our best, it all pales in comparison to Your loving Grace. Our treasure is not our cash, nor is it those who we lash. It is not our children for they are treasures of their own. Husbands it is not your wives, who you do not own. Wives, it's not your husbands who leave you alone. Our treasure is not the case of beer, we drink in our children's face, nor is it the excuses we use, for being in our mistresses' place. It is not the people we abuse, for no other reason than race. It is ourselves, with whom we have fallen out of place.

Children don't be afraid! The debts have already been paid. When the false prophets come, their lying demons will soar through their tongues. Since nothing but the truth can last, they too shall eventually pass. Classification, there is no measure, except when it comes to our pleasure. We like to put people in classes. We say they are smarter, if they wear glasses. The souls of the people, to God their all equal, Our judgments are none but our own. The faith of our fathers, the sins of our lovers, the patience of our teachers, the greed of our leeches; we say, "Thank you," to them all. For we've all taken that fall. But we have risen time and time again. Because through it all, God, you were there for us, Amen. Whether you forsake me, or take me off the street; whether straight, gay or lesbian we all pretend that God can't be our friend. Or is that the message that some Christians send?

Whether you're a basketball star, or if you only think that you are. When the seasons start, is that when your life begins, my friend? Is it with a new bottle of Gin; popping pills and casual sex, that you think you will win? Or will you discover the treasure within, one that's greater than sin. The key to your happiness is inside. So make the connection my friend, to your creator's gift that you can't hide. When you do you will find, that your treasure will blow your mind.

Section Eight

When you' ve lived a lie your whole life the truth may bring no satisfaction.

TITLE: *God has not forgotten you*

INSPIRATION: *I hosted a radio talk show called "The Promised Land" in the Virgin Islands from 2003-2005. One of my favorite episodes was part of a series we did in which we held an on-air poll where listeners called in to vote on the very controversial issue of whether Marijuana should be legalized in the Virgin Islands. 36% voted for the legalization of Marijuana and 55% voted against it. 9% were undecided. Not only did we see the results of our opinion poll, we revealed the insides of our country's soul. After several hateful calls, received both on- and off-air, directed towards our guest from the Rastafarian community. I revealed my intentions behind the topic of the program in the following piece, which concluded the series.*

The boat has been rocked; the pan of taboo issues has been knocked. They say that I have chosen the wrong venue, the wrong stage; to talk about issues we only see the fruits of, on the newspaper page. They cite me for being disrespectful to the nation; they say that my work is an abomination. These critics are from the Christian community, and if they are Christians what then, does that make me.

A display of democracy was met with a display of hate and bigotry, which came from the Christian community. The same Christians preach to you out on the street, but if you're hungry, they have nothing for you to eat. They give out tracks with messages of hope, but beyond the surface they act as if it was all a joke. They don't understand the words they say; they don't understand the prayers they pray. They have forgotten the meek and the mild; they have forgotten the hopeless child. Because he has locks in his head, when they see him, their eyes fill with hate, and turn red. They disapprove because they can't relate to his story; and they think their hateful behavior, brings God glory.

After the show, hurt by what had taken place, we became one with our guest and apologized for their disgrace. He expressed nothing but love and thankfulness, for what we had done. In that moment I realized, our work had just begun. We had built a bridge that wasn't there before, because we had laid down our reputations for something worth much more. We are not the same today and neither will he be, because we are now one in spirit, love and unity.

What the devil meant for evil, God turned around for good. Christians called with messages of hate, but today, those calls we celebrate. To those who have been forgotten by those who claim to represent God in our community, I will see to it that you are remembered, because when they remember you they will also remember me; because we have been made one, by their hate and bigotry.

We have built a bridge together, and we have suffered for this cause, just like those who came before us, those who fought unfair and hurtful laws. I have not forgotten the work that we must do; now to my friends dismissed and rejected, God has not forgotten you. He isn't blinded by your cannabis; nor is he turned off by your speaking style. And though you may smoke Marijuana, he still sees you as his child.

When will people learn how to love? That question's answer, I do not know. But I believe it must start with us, that we may set an example for others to follow. We must not hate as they do. In the way of love we must continue. Though we are tempted to sometimes slit our wrist; my friends who are like the sparrows please remember this: Though some Christians shoot you with their arrows, which they do in Jesus name. He has not forgotten you, and you must believe the same. They have forgotten God, they have left his love behind, and they have chosen to conform, to an ignorant state of mind. Will they be delivered, from their ignorant mentality? That is now the question; it's no longer Marijuana's legality.

TITLE: *They love you not*

INSPIRATION: *This piece was inspired after the bombshell that dropped on a church I used to attend, where the pastor was allegedly caught in bed with another man by his wife, who later divorced him.*

In writing this poem I dared to imagine myself as many different people in various circumstances who would want to know if God still loved them. People who have been overwhelmingly rejected in their respective communities, outside the extremes, however, everyday people want to know if God still loves them. For that's not the message they get from the Christians that judge them. They often wonder if they were up front and totally honest, with people in their lives who claim to love them unconditionally, how long before their love and the condition exchange hands. How long before they stop calling you to make plans? The answer all too often, is not long. Not long before they, all of a sudden, have so many things to do. Not long before, on the list of those who are important, the least of which is you. Must you then not wonder if what you have is real, with those who claim to love you, when they know not what you feel? They only accept you on the surface, without the layers peeled.

Life is not the simple fairytale, we learned about in Sunday school. We are not unconditionally loved, to test that, just try and break a rule. God has creative ways, to show us up in our hypocrisy; it wasn't but a few months ago, that we questioned a pastor's sexuality. What if he came forward and confirmed what many believed to be true. Would we be able to love him, the way God would ask us to? We cannot overcome indifference in our community, because we do not possess love in its true capacity. We can love unconditionally when there are no conditions, but how strong does our love stand, when someone challenges our traditions?

We have the opportunity to rise higher every day, but we keep tripping on the steps that we're supposed to take along the way. We have the lives we live, for that's all that we can see, because from where we stand, there's no better we that we can be. We judge the man who does not live his life according to our plan, because we think he has to change to be deserving of our love and be a man. Instead it is he who offers us a truly remarkable gift. It is to get beyond his faults, which only true love can lift. It is not our job to change our fellow man, but to love him and in doing so, bring to light God's own plan. We have been distracted by sin's illusion. It is time we refocus on love's conclusion. We cannot live our lives with joy, unless we get it clear, that the only way to heaven, is to let love erase our fear. Life does not allow us, to go forward unaware. What we neglect to face outside, at home we'll soon see it there...

TITLE: *We didn't know love*

INSPIRATION: *This piece represents everything that every child, regardless of their age, wants to say to their parents. The only way to heal the disconnection is to listen and therefore understand what is really being said. We are losing and have lost too many children who in someway have given up on themselves. They didn't know love from their parents and didn't learn how to love from anyone else.*

I don't know how to say help,
So I scream and I cry
I'm hoping that you'll understand, as I throw things and watch them fly
Though I can't seem to find a way to say
I must try, because this pain won't seem to go away

I didn't know how to say help,
You say you showed me love, when you hit me with the belt
If that's your version of love, I hate the way it felt
Because I didn't know what to say, you left me with a welt
To make matters worse, the look in your eye made me melt.

You responded to my actions, which you couldn't understand
You thought that I was saying, that I think that I'm a man
You were so over-confident, in what you didn't know
Encouraged by those who like to say, "See, I told you so"

It's all because I didn't know how to say help
I didn't know how to show you my needs
And you misinterpreted my deeds
You say I'm rude and a disgrace, to the family name
And to look at me even brings you, feelings of great shame
If you say that you love me, why do I feel this pain?
You say that love is suppose to feel good
I wish that your love could

What I now believe is, that you are confused
Maybe your parents mistreated you, that is why you now
abuse
I have come to understand, many things because of one
thing I did not know how to do
Which was to say, all I wanted was to be loved by you

I'm sorry I couldn't make it clear
I just wanted to know that you really cared and you were
near
I see my friends die trying to say the same thing
But no one understands the songs that they sing
So they go and join gangs and clicks
Looking for a love that sticks
A love that stays around
Trying to replace the daddy or mommy they never had or
never found

In their search for love they die it seems
Along with them their hopes and dreams
We forego the wisdom of love when we neglect to show it
But we have no hope, if we do not know it
Dear God, it does make me sad
If I could help save but one, my heart would be glad
Just one or two with what gifts you gave me
To be of service to you and help set the people free...

TITLE: *A note of sobriety*

INSPIRATION: *There are so many predators out there waiting to take advantage of the opportunities our weaknesses leave, for them to practice to deceive. It is our very nature as human beings, that makes us want to belong, and believe in something. For many of us religion fills this void, it gave me peace, and then it was destroyed. I came to learn how powerful these predators could be, even inside the religious community. I found myself in the midst of a cult; they misled me and added injury to insult. They tried to change me in ways that never felt right, and I obliged because I never knew a love for which I didn't have to fight. When I decided that the price to conform was too high to pay, I learned that their love was as untrue as anything they had to say. I wrote this piece after I got out, but not before they tried to leave*

me with permanent doubt. They told me I'd amount to
nothing if I left them behind, but somehow I found the
strength of mind. I broke away and never pined. If I
hadn't departed, I'd still be blind...

Let the transformation begin, pretending days have already
begun to come to an end; and what will be will be, the
future is still a mystery to me. But there are some who claim
to know the story that has yet to unfold. They say it's by the
Holy Ghost they have been told. But I ask for forgiveness
for their soul, even though taking advantage was their goal.
They used my trust to deceive me, but I take what they
say now with a note of sobriety. Indeed it makes me sad,
how people use love for something bad. They use trust
to tell lies. They are master manipulators of the fabric of
trust, woven with wool to pull over your eyes. Having been
liberated today, I no longer hang onto the words they say. I
don't need their prayers for me to feel alright, nor do I need
their affirmations to sleep at night.

My faith lets me take it light, now that my unfounded fears
have taken flight. I won't look back or make apologies for
my decisions, or the truth, which has influenced it, delivered
with precision. The truth that only I must know, it is the
truth that reveals now why I had to go. What will be will
be, but the past is no longer a mystery to me. It's over now;
you should let it be, because you can't change it because you
can't change me. What you are doing is wrong, but you use

God to defend it strong. So you carry on with being 'right,' since that's more important to you than seeing the light. I can honestly say this hour breeds a brand new day, because I have made a choice to no longer live that way. You dare to question my will to make a decision that I know is right, because in your infinite 'wisdom' you can't even see the light. Maybe it's not for you to see; you don't know everything concerning me. I will trust Him who has created me, in the face of my closest enemy. Everyday they pray for me, with their false intentions, and everyday I will pray to be, delivered from their pretentions. Lies they say are secrets, that they cannot mention. But I say what you're telling me, is simply your invention. When we finish praying we both say, "Amen," but they say my prayers will go unanswered because of sin. I intend, however, to keep on trusting Him.

When being right is more important than doing what is right, there's something really wrong. But unfortunately that is the direction, many believers have gone. They will be 'right,' but in the wrong place. They will be winning, but in the wrong race. They'll have strong arguments, but in the wrong case. They will have the right answers, but to the wrong questions. They will have the right ideas, but the wrong perceptions. They may have started with the right intention, but they no longer trust God, for the right direction. Whatever they have to say now is alright with me, because He taught me to disregard it without even a bit of anxiety.

Section Nine

Sometimes it's wise to be silent, and sometimes you need to be silent to be wise.

TITLE: *Along came a skeleton*

INSPIRATION: *In this piece I wanted to express
my disgust for the appetite that exists within our society
for gossip. It's a damn shame how willing some of us
are to spread ugliness regarding others. When someone
is violated in such a public manner especially within a
small community the effects are all the more devastating.
Yet the saddest things about the situation are the lack of
compassion and the fact that some people actually seem
to delight in the misfortune of others.*

Rumors, rumors, oh the consumers watching and waiting
for an encore. They are not satisfied with the truth, especially
when a lie promises so much more. A promise is a comfort
to a fool; I thought you learned that in Sunday school. Yet
you still search for gore. Look at you, you're drooling, and
stooling all over the floor. All you eat at best is someone
else's mess. You thrive on their hurt. You obsess with what's
underneath someone's skirt. You capitalize on someone
else's dirt, and you love the filth of the afterbirth. You want
a reason to think of yourself as more, when all you are, is
a carnivore. A flesh eating beast, oh the smell of the farts
you release. They come from indigestion of other people's
business, there's no question. It has become your religion,
because spreading hurtful gossip is your decision.

Rumors aside, Lord we abide... In prayer for those who

have fallen from grace, to judge them it is not our place. I know their enemies salivate with great sensation. They say no one could recover from this devastation. And not only do they wish for your resignation, they expect your ultimate ruination. Some of the best things, though, come from dirt. Thank God for our Earth, and how can we heal unless we hurt? How can we give birth to wisdom, unless we feel pain? If we are never tested, how can we know the meaning of our Saviors name? Sometimes our skeletons come out of our closets before we do. They have chosen a different venue, and even without tongues they tell of our issues. We try to live as if they don't exist, but sometimes they come forth, in ways we cannot dismiss. The life we created in the public view has been destroyed for a reason. It is time for our nation's healing, for change, it is now the season.

Let the skeletons be free, as they come forth from the pew and sanctuary. Do you have the courage to be still while they walk, and can you remain seated, and listen to the truth as they talk? I'm sorry we have been interrupted, by a bulletin from CNN; it says your skeletons are no longer in the closet my friend. As a result the community is enraged, but this is an opportunity... Can you feel the winds of change?

We are sorry for any inconvenience we may have caused. We now return to our regularly scheduled gossip that was paused. Bring your skeletons out to the national day of prayer. What a day of healing, we could all share. Pain would turn into power, and our rumor mills would seize up within the hour. Instead of our lips flapping in the breeze, we would all bruise up our knees. Because instead of vicious rumors in the air, there would be the sweet sound of honest prayer. And when we get the urge to point our fingers and say, "He, she, he." We'd feel a nudge from our skeletons knee. They'd tell us not to laugh at others, because you know you've still got me.

I believe if we let our skeletons free, then we will open up an opportunity. To see the love of God in operation, and no longer wearing our Christianity like a decoration. We will be naked before each other, just like God sees me and you. Naked with no symbols saying, "What would Jesus do?" Naked with no denomination labels. Naked at our own dinner tables. Would you run through the streets naked in Jesus name? No? Then you shouldn't be so willing to strip someone of their good name. If we could look at the skeletons of others with compassion, we would realize that like ours, they are created in the very same fashion. They are our own sons and our daughters, our own sisters and our brothers, our own mothers and fathers they are our demons and our bothers. They are our own ministers and our pastors, our public representatives, and our personal disasters. But most importantly of all, they all are our neighbors. And they deserve the very best of our labors. As you do yourselves, Love your neighbor. Stop using your tongue as your saber. And love them with their skeletons too, because despite your own, God still loves you.

TITLE: *Home sweet home*

INSPIRATION: *I was inspired to write this piece after a close friend shared with me what life was like in his house having to keep the peace between two parents that didn't seem to like each other anymore.*

I see the sadness in their eyes, though they work hard for us not to recognize; Mom and Dad both dry their eyes before coming through the front door and perpetuating their guise. We wash dishes, clean our rooms, sweep and mop the floor, but keeping peace in our house is our biggest chore. Our parents don't like each other any more, and they don't love us like they did before. We all use to cuddle together in the living room where silence was ok, now in our house it's like the war before Judgment day. Home sweet home that is what our welcome mats say, but if that is true why do our parents cry outside over them every day? They always say education is the key, but they have it and are still not happy. I don't want their life for me. I have never known such misery. I often wonder if this is how life is meant to be. But that's not how it seems when I watch TV.

The situation is basically the same at my friends' house next-door, same story but on a different floor. The same script, but with a different cast. They are rich, but sadness seems to know no class. We all too often live over our parents' past. We can't seem to shake the spells that they cast. And what we hate most about them, it seems we become. How do we escape the curses of the families we come from?

(Five Years Later)

I'm in college now, trying to get an education; my professor always says with one we will have the tools to change our Nation. Going to college is turning out to be a great experience for me; I don't know where I learn more, in the classroom or dormitory. My roommates all echo the lives they come from in some way; some of them are so mysterious, others, it seems, have too much to say. Some you just have to learn how to ignore, before we change our nation, we first have to learn how to sweep the floor. Some of my roommates think they already know it all. No one can tell them about life, share advice or guide them away from hitting a wall. We wonder why they are so arrogant until their parents come to visit. Then the revelation is quite exquisite.

It's funny how we become our past, I'm learning more about that subject in my psychology class. The apple doesn't fall far from the tree, but if you see an apple that gets up and starts running... that's me. They tell us we can be anything we want to be, why then do we choose a familiar destiny? Sometimes we become what we hate the most, possessed it seems by our parent's ghost. One young man described the other day in class, how his father kicked his mother's ass. He described a man he said he would never be, in tears. But it seems he was that man already, living out his fears. We all saw what happened in the courtyard; in a fit of rage he slapped his girl friend, very hard. We later heard she suffered a dislocated jaw, but she still went back to him after the stars she saw; I guess she didn't learn anything from that slap, or is it what she learned about herself that keeps her coming back.

We are all here for a better future they say, but what I see is the past being lived over every day. I went back home for Thanksgiving Day, where those same welcome mats still prominently lay. My brother is now in the room where I use to be, my Mom and Dad are still together in their misery. Mom says they stay together in the name of family, they must stick together religiously. What's the point of that Mom, if you hate each other? What good does that do, if you stopped being my Mother? Now we hate who we are, because of you two. College may help us find work, but we are constantly blue. Though we may be able to escape poverty, who will teach us how to escape misery?

This article is dedicated to those of us apples who didn't fall far from the tree, but then realized we had to get up and run, in order to choose our own destiny. Though the road is harder for those like you and I, we must run on else we daily die. As we shed the skin of our ancestral past, we blaze trials to places they never passed. As we experience salvation from the demons our forefathers bore, in this new day we can become so very much more. Though life be ordinary for others, you see... it can be extraordinary for you and for me. You may not have fallen far from the tree, but if you run on, nothing limits your destiny. Run! Run like you never ran before, and may the winds of change meet you as you soar. Your future is brighter than you could ever realize. Remember He will be with you on the day that you rise!

TITLE: *A dying man's eulogy*

INSPIRATION: *I have come to the realization that the only enemy we really need to be concerned about is the enemy within. This piece was inspired by a sermon preached by a young man named Courtney Jones at the New Life Baptist Church on February 8th 2004. I dedicate it to all my brothers like Courtney who aspire to be sons of God.*

Love is my disease, I prayed for it and when it came I

prayed that it would leave. If I knew what I prayed for, if I knew what God paid for. You must be careful what you pray, because of my prayers, I die a little now each day. But don't feel bad for me though, I must die so these demons will let me go. I've lived with them for oh, so long. I know their names and I know their songs. They cry out in pain, and tell me that they hate when I call out His name. They rebuke me because loving God is my conviction. I can understand better now, the pain of my Fathers crucifixion. He died because He loved me, and so I could be free from thee enemy. If I am to truly be His son, I too must die to overcome.

Love is my disease and some days I still pray that it would leave. But I'm learning to pray a different prayer, one only a son of Him, who was crucified, could share. For it's the pain of my affliction that makes me say God I can't do this. I can't go through this! Then it's the love of my conviction that makes me pray, "Lord help me die a little every day; love me despite the things my demons make me say. Ease me from the pain they cause me, please. As I lose the battle with this disease. Every day I watch hurt, hate, and envy leave, all because I now truly believe. Forgive me for how I may act at times, the power of these demons have a strong influence on my mind. Like father, like son you died for me, now the process of my death will change my history. One more thing, Lord, before I conclude this prayer, my brother is also afflicted with this disease we share. And he believes the pain is too much for him to bear. For him, give me the strength to be there. Because the part of me that still needs to die, doesn't really care. So hear me Lord, for this is my prayer. It's the prayer that dying men always pray; the prayer that I will pray, as I die a little every day.

This is what my eulogy reads: I must die because only when I die can certain goals be achieved. Rejoice for me. Don't let my apparent suffering sadden thee, because when I die, I will rise again and be free. Not as I am now, but in a very different skin. You can't kill a dead man again and again. So no matter what evil does, no matter what weapons it forms, no matter what confusion it causes I'll be able to whether the effects of the storm. When I die and rise again it will be in love like my Father did way back when. So that His children would be saved from original sin.

So as I die each day and pray, the prayers that dying men always pray, I do so because I truly want to meet my Father some day. I do so for my brother's sake, because I can't love him, if this step I do not take. I can't leave him behind because my love for him won't let me. Although his demons make him right now, reject me; I must still fight for him because this fight will perfect me. The position in which it puts me leaves me to choose, whether I will die for him, or let my brother lose. I have to die so that he can die and then live. I have to be willing to lose my life so he would have his to give. That's why I cry, shake and shiver, because another life depends on mine to deliver. There is no greater task than to love thy own brother. And that task also means to love one another. But what it really means for us to do that is to die a death from which there is no coming back. Am I willing to die? It is a question still struggling to answer am I?   But I do answer a little each day, as I pray the prayers dying men pray.

Section Ten

I was changed by the service of others, and I was transformed, as I rendered my own.

TITLE: *Confessions of a tollbooth cashier*

INSPIRATION: *For several months I worked at the Georgia 400 Toll Plaza as a cashier. The following pieces were all inspired by the various experiences I had with the public in that capacity. I wrestled with the decision to write this piece for a while, but it was like a literary ghost that haunted me much like the voice of my inner child. I knew that it was a story, which had to be told, and that I had to surrender to the spirit to of let it unfold...*

Toll booth virgin

One of the first things I realized once I started working at the Georgia 400 toll Plaza was that in many ways my experiences there would be metaphoric of the journey that is life. I am told that over 3 million vehicles come through the toll Plaza each month, and who knows how many of these faces I see. What I do know is that with each face there's an expression and behind every expression there's a story that their energy is telling, and although they come and go they leave behind hints of the world in which they're dwelling. This is a story that is so compelling, that I find myself often retelling. It is one that has taught me so very much. Tossing quarters is simple enough, but this has been a front row seat in a sociology class that has been really tough. For the first couple months the toll booth virgin was me, and Oh my God, I can't believe some of the things that my eyes have shown me. And so here goes the story...

The look of judgment

There is no harsher judge of us than he whose reflection lies in our own mirror. Although I have the pleasure of being a citizen of these United States, I spent a significant part of my childhood living in the British Virgin Islands with my grandparents whose love and affection wasn't as present as their displeasure and judgment. So I'm very familiar with the look of judgment, after all I spent years looking at my self and my life through those eyes. Through those eyes all I could see, was a self I didn't want to be and a life I didn't want to live.

Today, after turning self-hatred into hope and finding a purpose for my pain, I no longer look at my self or my life through the eyes of judgment or those of shame. And because this is true, I can stand in the face of judgment and take his 50 cents and be undefined by his thoughts concerning my lack of worth. Or, his looks that suggest my life equates to dirt. Or his question – Are you going to pick that up? Because he dropped his 50 cents outside the bin, too busy pitying the state he perceives I'm in.

The look or the ways of judgment are no strangers to me, but I stand strong in the faces of judgment driving through these lanes, you see. Every day I am confronted with the self-reflection that their car windows display. It is now one of non-judgment, I am happy to say. I am not perfect in my own eyes and I never wish to be, but I am learning to see my self and others through Gods eyes as the process of growth continues in me. When I see the eyes of judgment looking back at me, I think not in terms of race because I don't define my self or others by the color of their face.

What I see however is a human being blinded by an illusion supported by a system of paradigms built on mistruths and stereotypes, therefore locking them into a conclusion that is incorrect. I am hardly hurt by their inability to see me correctly for a brief moment in time. The thought that lingers with me is how tragic it would be, if they lived their whole lives without ever being free, from the prison of their own paradigms. Often, it is what we do to ourselves, not others that are the worst of our crimes.

"Don't you wish you went to school instead of being out here tossing quarters?" This rhetorical question asked of by someone making an assumption about the cashier's education level shows that the look of judgment is sometimes as stated.

Paying it backwards

I've been a car enthusiast long before I understood that some people use cars as symbols of status. From where I sit in the tollbooth as a cashier at the Georgia 400 Toll Plaza I recognize the marquee of many automobiles before I can see their drivers. While the emblem may speak to the class of the car, it says nothing about the class of the person(s) it has carried thus far. I so often wished that classy cars came with classy people, and maybe their owners do too. Unfortunately, while money can buy class in cars, it cannot buy class in you.

What truly sets people apart is not the nature of their cars, but the nature of their heart. I'm always moved by those who say "pay for the person behind me" with an energy that finds me wanting to explore, the depth of people's kindness which inspires others to do more. Every now and then someone pays their toll with a five or a ten and says pass it on my friend, and I get the joy of using their change to make a change in someone else's day. I get to enjoy the surprise of unsuspecting commuters as they discover that someone else has paid their way. I love to be a part of it, and see how it so often makes their day. It's not about the 50 cents, but about uncommon kindness that defies the logic of common sense.

There are those who believe it or not just don't get it, they don't understand why someone would want to pay their way. "I don't know them and they don't know me" they would say. Instead of just saying thank you, they miss the message and the opportunity to pass it on; but I never miss the message for it is one I intimately know. I will never forget the day when a lady got out of the back of her grandson's car to look me in the eyes to tell me she didn't have the toll fee, as I saw and felt the depth of her honesty I told her "it's on me", and what a spectacle she made at the toll, as she gave me a hug that left an impression on my soul. First class people may not always drive up in first class cars, and they may not always be able to pay the toll, but I am careful to recognize and respect them no matter what they drive up in, because what they drive up as is a first class soul.

Is it rude to make a request from someone before you acknowledge the person you're making the request from? Apparently many folks traveling through the Georgia 400 Toll Plaza don't think so.

A receipt please

The question that is most often asked by the commuters passing through the Georgia 400 Toll Plaza everyday is one that is often asked without the acknowledgment of the tollbooth cashier behind the window. The person that is expected to reach for falling quarters while taking a strangers orders. It is a question that represents many, and it is one, which I think about as I count each and every filthy penny. I count the many dollar bills that are so badly worn, like my emotions that inspire the questions between which I am so badly torn. Questions like: 'why was I born?' Certainly not to be scorned for making an honest living, or to be a servant for customers who believe they are always right, but they stand in the wrong shoes to see the light.

Can I have a receipt? It is the question often asked with condescending undertones to which I often do not reply. If manners were like a drink of water or a breath of fresh air, I'd have as much luck as a pilgrim in a desert hoping to find them there. Yet it is the quest of every pilgrim on a journey to be seen as someone worthy in a world that may not be quite convinced, we want a receipt for something more than 50 cents. We want a receipt for the hopes our hearts hold. We are people that matter! We have stories that go untold, and dreams we dare not speak of for the fear of what someone might say; who are we to want more out of life for the debts that we pay?

A receipt is an acknowledgment of where we've come from and where we hope to go. It says that you have paid your dues, which you hope to recoup someday, and you should be able to live the life you choose. That is what our tears travel down our faces to say, as we work for all these bills we have to pay. And the dream is that one day, there will no longer be an outstanding balance, a day where we get paid not for our warm bodies but our talents. This is the dream of many hard working Americans every day, to live for the work they love, so that they will never have to work another day. A receipt please, that is what is due as we continue to work to make our dreams come true.

Myths, Facts and Solutions @ the GA 400 Toll Plaza

Myth: Holding your horn for extended periods of time gets you quicker service.

Fact: You're more likely to be ignored as you make a fool of your self in front of other drivers.

Solution: Consider actually behaving like a human being, get out of your car and see the nearest cashier.

Myth: Cashiers will pay your toll if you wink at them, and tell them how good they look.

Fact: Ah No honey, this is a tollbooth your powers don't work here.

Solution: Consider just actually looking at the bottom of your bag or man purse, rather than embarrassing your self any further by begging.

Myth: If I am entirely to far from the toll booth when I drive up, someone will fetch my money for me so I don't have to get out of my car.

Fact: Tollbooths are stationary. Enough said!

Solution: Consider using that round thingy called your steering wheel to direct your vehicle closer to the tollbooth as you drive up.

Travelling through

We may all be traveling on the same roads, but we are on many different journeys. We are traveling to destinations that we may never see, because we failed to pack what was needed to make the trip. We may not have everything we will need when we are starting out, but in order to succeed we must rise to the occasion when the occasion arises. Our needs are what our journey realizes. It is the need for a steady paycheck that brings the Georgia 400 Toll Plaza cashiers there. It is what we do not need that makes this job more difficult than some of us can bear. It is the many nasty stares, but unfortunately too often they do not stop there. We've been called niggers, we've been called bitches and some of us have remained silent for fear of the doctor's stitches.

When I started out on the journey that led me to

this place, I made many stops before here that prepared me for what I'd face. I'm glad no one ever tells us how difficult the journey would be, because the fear that would grip us, would keep us from becoming the people we need to be. There are some things that I have been through, which I wouldn't choose to go through again, but giving up now is not something, I even can comprehend. I've decided to run on because I want to see what the end will be, and I want to know that the final destination, was worth the trouble it's caused me.

We may all be traveling on the same roads, but we each have our own unique battles to face, battles that bring us to any given place. Life is not a race; it is more about keeping pace. There are no short cuts, for the things that we must see, to become the kind of people, we all strive to be. There are no alternate routes, on the road to victory. We must ultimately be tested, in order to have a testimony. This is what I come to proclaim today, it is what gets me to my feet to say. I am here, and all my life's lessons stand with me. And because of the wisdom those lessons carry, I can say with absolute certainty, that I have never been so free.

The journey is long and there is a lot of work left for us to do. So, this is my prayer for all of you: That your visions for your lives, become so clear, that you burn a path to success, through your fear. In order to enjoy success tomorrow we must work for it today. Your faithfulness will be rewarded all along the way.

TITLE: *This Side of Crazy*

INSPIRATION: *Who ever said, "Art imitates life," was certainly correct because, like so much of my work, this piece is a prime example of it. I wrote this piece while at work as a security officer, because of a need to express my mounting frustrations about the culture which existed within this particular work place. I was an alien among co-workers whose only motivation in life was money. I couldn't be content with the idea of giving up my dreams to be a corporate slave. Not when the blood of a passionate artist runs through my veins.*

I came in to work late again, unexcited about a job I have no future in. Working along side people who are overly satisfied, with their $35,000 salaries, they have so much pride. They justify their contentment by comparing themselves with others who make much less. Those who can't afford the cars they drive or their style of dress. They have become a corporate slave, they are told how to think and they are punished when they do not behave. Somehow none of it is worth it to me, to have a mind of my own, yet be controlled by someone who thinks I have no power and I'm only worth eleven bucks an hour. Maybe underneath it all, I believe that too, although I am working on making that belief untrue. That's the only work I am excited to do. My co-workers tell me that I am crazy and that, I don't deny. They are the ones that have been offered a bill of goods and they chose it, to buy. I am David against the corporate Goliath, seen as crazy because of where my faith lieth. They have been bought for a price higher than what they value themselves to be, and sold for a price that will never be good enough for me. Who do you think you are? That is one among the questions they ask. But comprehending the answer is, for them, too great a task. They can't see the vision of me, because theirs is one of mediocrity. Is it any wonder, that that is how they'd be. Since, as they'll proudly tell you, they define themselves by their salary.

If I am crazy, then this is the crazy I am going to happily be. Crazy enough to believe that race, is not a factor for me. Crazy enough to dream of a life, for which I do not have to sell my soul to acquire. Crazy enough to rebel, against society's mediocre standards as my goal to retire. You have to be real crazy to step out on faith, for that is something to which sane folks cannot relate. They preach, sing, and talk about it in Church all Sunday long, but where is it, when Sunday's gone. Crazy is what you have to be, to live a life to which even your family does not agree. Crazy is a solo hymn, by the time you get to the chorus all your friends you won't find them. Crazy, well it's sometimes a narrow road, with deep valleys where the only light comes from within. It's also sometimes a mountaintop, where the journey there, takes all you've got. Crazy is despite hearing what the entire world has to say, knowing that you're really not that way. Crazy is to know that no matter what they try to sell you, through good lies they try to tell you, that you are still the best thing that you've got.

Crazy is to believe that you can fight a battle with your fists to your side, and turning the other cheek to your enemy so that they may see the heart of your pride. Thank you Dr. Martin Luther King, you laid down your life and forced society to rethink everything. "I have dream" that's what you said, not so long ago. There were those who said you were crazy, and I am glad that it was so. I want to be crazy just like you, to have a dream worth dying for to make it come true. If I am crazy then I am proud to be, because it's all crazy, but this side of crazy is me.

TITLE: *Hood Rich*

INSPIRATION: *The irony in this money obsessed culture we live in, is that no matter how much stuff we buy to fill the void of emptiness we have inside, we still end up feeling cheap in the end. We have heard that money can't buy us love, but do you know, Ms. Thang, that hair extensions don't come with self-esteem? Do you have enough brain cells left Brotha Man to comprehend that our problems don't go away after smoking weed?*

Brotha Man...

We walk tall, we ride high, and in the finest gear we look good in the arms of the honey who's dear. But who are you without your money? If you can't buy everyone drinks, are your jokes still funny? Seems like you got a new car every year, and as fast as your wheels spin you are still going nowhere. You smoke that blunt, because you say it makes you feel high. But please don't front, we both know you're living a lie. You ask me if I know what you mean, but will you, my brother, ever see beyond the smoke screen?

We are losing you in great numbers every day; because you want to live the lifestyle, the music videos portray. They tell you that your popularity depends on how many curse words you say, and your manhood is measured, by how many girls you lay. I heard you say you're sleeping with her mother too, you ever wonder what kind of woman would want to be with you? How many kids you got now? You're not even sure. Yeah, you think you're the man, doing it hardcore. Sit for a minute and listen, while your girl braids your hair. Let this message linger, your manhood is full of hot air. Right now you're flying high, but can you survive the fall from the lie? Your money can support the illusion, but what will save you from its conclusion?

Ms. Thang...

How much money did you spend at the hairdresser today? Yes I'm talking to you don't act like you don't understand the words that I say. I'm tired of the games that you play. You act like you're so hard... to get, but the brothers in the hood say you're the easiest one... don't fret. You just got to be real, why you spending so much money fixing your hair when you don't got no inner appeal. You think them brothers like you, nah, they just like how you feel. They only call you when they can't eat from the main dish, that's for real. You are like Mc Donald's; good to drive through, but no one values you. You're value meal might as well be free, because you just giving it out to everybody. Yet you cutting style with me girl please, you better ask somebody. Laurel, Mary Kay, Trojan, those are all names you know, but what does your name stand for, in the hood you're just a "ho".

I just want you to understand, that for your life, God has a greater plan. He created you to be more, why do you insist on being a whore. Consider this to be your meeting at the well, and listen carefully because this lesson I won't retell. Consider this the pebble before the stone falls, shut off that phone before another man calls. I can't believe you are pregnant again, you need to stop acting like a clothes pin. When your head's closed, your legs stay open. You might be a woman someday, but not with the current behavior you display. You can live a different life today, not one that's filled with dismay. You can be a queen on the inside too, when you start to value you. This is how the battle will be won, it's as plain as the rising sun. We must confront our demons where they lie, and the battle ground, is inside you and I. We can only live the lives we are able to see, we can only be the people we imagine ourselves to be. When we begin to see ourselves from a different point of view, the lives we live shall also be brand new.

Section Eleven

Sometimes we call people friends, not because they have been to us, but because we have been to them.

TITLE: *The results are in*

INSPIRATION: *My three-day stay in the ICU (intensive care unit) began after a fun day with friends at the beach. I had an unknown lingering medical issue that caused severe fatigue that was exacerbated especially after strenuous activity. After a challenging competition of track and field on the sand, we found ourselves in a rush not to the finish line but the emergency room after I collapsed. As the truth about my mysterious medical condition came to light, so did the truth about a close female friend with a lying tongue. Apparently the time had come for all these mysteries to be undone. The knowledge that would come was that my heart was broken in more ways than one.*

The results are in
It is confirmed I do not pretend
And in these times of uncertainty
Circles of trust are shrinking around me
The true nature of my friend's loyalty
Is a question that has arisen lately

I knew something was wrong
In my heart I felt it strong
No evidence on paper
Faith getting thin like vapor
If I knew that she'd lie
I would have taped her so she couldn't deny

The results are in
I now feel validated within
I'm no longer haunted by the suggestion
The truth I know, they no longer question
And here they go with their prayers of healing
They do not know that their fate I am sealing

Compassion is the key to loving others without condition
It is work, though, bringing that to fruition
And although things sometimes don't turn out right
Family and friends are worth the fuss and fight
Crying tears day and night
For our relationships are of the faulty type

Compassion teaches me that despite their frailty
Their deceptive ways, their lack of loyalty
God says to me, love them despite what their conditions be
And the fact that they have no honest identity
Doesn't make them an unlovable entity.

So with compassion I pray the prayer of the wise
Lord let me love my enemy with open eyes
Let not their deceptive ways be hidden
Give me strength to fight the forbidden
As they come to see if I am dead or living
Let me rise above and be forgiving

The hope is that they'd come to Thee
If I can let thine love shine through me
And look beyond what the details be
To embrace a profound possibility
Experiencing a love through which we see
The world so differently

What's the purpose of Christianity?
To be mocked by its own insanity?
Or to be locked into a twisted mentality,
That some followers say, is best for me?
Is it merely used as a cloak,
By puppeteers who take it for a joke?

The results are in after three days in the ICU
The truth is that I now see you
A leaky valve in my heart is true
Doctors can't see that it's broken, too
That's the truth I already knew
It is longing for a love that's due

TITLE: *Those days*
INSPIRATION: *This piece was inspired by the good times I had with friends while growing up in New York City.*

Conversations
Heart palpitations
Stomach irritations
Mixed communications
Heart break patience, Celebrations
That came from understanding human relations

The commonness we knew
We no longer do the things we use to
That common bird has flown
We're too big now, too grown
And what has flown with the common fowl,
Is the love of those days which are gone now

What a web of grief we weave
Because of the love we no longer perceive
The days of good morning afternoons we did lose
Along with those of being irresponsible for
what we choose

Those days I remember are filled with
memories of true friends
I thought those days would never end.
And somehow forever has nothing to do with time
For it's not a measure of what we would find

Those days I can't believe they're gone
Now a moment of silence, for those days
have made me strong
I used to think about tomorrow
I used to wish for it with sorrow
But all I have is today
And the memories of love and fun that stay

For my friends have passed away from this present time
They now dwell in the silent passages of my mind
I so much miss our communion
I dreamt once of a reunion
With my friend who knew what those days meant
Where what had gone, returned from
where it had been sent

Each day now that passes
Leaves me with an appreciation that surpasses
All the smallness, which use to bother me
I have risen above in order to be stress free

I've learned that gratitude can be an aid
In celebration of the progress we've made

Those days have not let me down
Instead they have led me to many truths that are profound
There's one in particular that comes to mind
Worry is a waste of time...

Section Twelve

I use to hate myself but I don't anymore. I was walking towards the cliff, but now I'm walking towards the shore.

TITLE: *Our enemies as well*

INSPIRATION: *I wrote this piece in honor of all the people that help to create circumstances that make our lives more difficult than we'd like. What they don't realize is that they give us opportunities to become better, stronger and wiser as well.*

We are our enemies' friend, when we decide not to let hate ascend. Our hope as a people is in our ability to love. Even at times when such things are unheard of. We create pestilence in our children, when love and appreciation is not given. Then we can't see it as the reason, we out live them and they die out of season.

We are our enemies' friend when we decide to fight for unity until the end. What friends are for, is a sure bet more, than what our enemies can lend. No diamonds or gems, no Lexus or Benz, is worth an early journey's end. When death becomes our hero, the Devil becomes our friend. But in darkness there is no light, no friendship, only fright. Love will live where life is, but where strife goes, death follows. As a heart without love is hollow, death becomes it tomorrow. As death plunges its hateful knife, it engulfs yet another life.

Whether our prayers are prayers of happiness or sorrow, they must be prayed today in order to affect tomorrow. Whether they are for a friend or foe, for our mothers and fathers, or for those of us who have parents they don't know. Whether they are for the singer down the street, or the homeless man who can hardly stand on his feet; the doctor who is not so nice or so neat; the chef who can't cook but there's nowhere else to eat. Whether they are for the children who are abused, misused, and consequently, confused; Our prayers must flow to heal the bruised.

Could it be you, who needs the prayer? Has the pain gotten too much for you to bear? Do you no longer feel better when you swear? Have you stopped praying because you believe that all your wrongs have caused God to turn a deaf ear? What about all the lies that you share? Have you lied so much, you no longer know how to be sincere? What happens now that your sexual escapades have left you naked and bare?

No matter how much makeup you put on, you can't hide with that fake smile your scorn. You may have more money than they do, but you'll end up needing them to join you in prayer to ask God's pardon upon you. No matter what the politicians may say, we'll all see who God votes for on judgment day. We are our enemy's friend, when we decide that it's for them we will pray. When we realize where our true enemy lies, and as silent tears fill our eyes. In our prayers we shall fervently say. God bless my family and friends until their journey ends, and remember our enemies as well.

TITLE: *What will we do for them?*

INSPIRATION: *I am the child whose voice I wanted to be heard. I wanted my pain, hurt and fears to be acknowledged as something other than absurd. I wanted to be validated by anyone, really, that would, especially when I believed the lie that there was nothing about me that was good. I've been called an activist for children over the years, because I am the child that I see through other's tears. I am the child I see in others; they are my sisters and my brothers. They are my friends and my family and I am standing and speaking up for them now, like I wanted someone to do for me somehow.*

A tear for all the times we tried to make up lines, we say we can't be there, for one to love and care. A breath, for all we've left behind, to die a silent death; and so it goes on and on, like no one sees the wrong.

When will we realize, and see our living lies? We live in such a way, that death defines our day. The children must be strong, we blame them for all the wrong; no wonder they destruct, filled with all that muck.

Yet we expect them to make it in life, with chains of hurt and strife. How can they succeed when in their hearts they bleed, all because of the love they need?

How can they breathe the breath of life, when death is in their hearts and minds? How do they pray when they display the spirit of dismay? They need our love to help them find their way.

Pastors, if you could understand it takes a helping hand. Don't form another church, and leave the children in the lurch. What we need is unity, but no more pastor friends you see. No more religion, what we need is a decision, a means to an end of all derision.

We don't need another religion to begin, a religion I must sign a paper to be in – because it's not enough that Jesus be my friend.

I feel like the deal to give up my free will is my end. And that religion has too little to do with God, and too much to do with how much money I spend.

It is nothing but the decision, for the division, that has blurred the vision, of unity. If in our heart we are divided, we will never be united, and forever separated in a religious society we created.

The heaven we sing about, the streets of gold we read about, we will never see. For the least we do unto God's children, we also do unto Him. How can heaven's beauty we see, if we can't love one another and be religion free? For in religion there is no unity.

When children are born, we teach them to scorn, after those who live differently. We show them how indifferent we can be. Then they learn that difference is not exclusive to strangers, when it shows up in the family.

The children are just acting out what we teach them to be. Just look at all the "politicality" and religious "fanaticality." Just look and see if you aren't a part of the devil mentality. What message are we sending, to the children about who we are? When they talk about it in the media, we say they've gone too far. We don't want them to talk, because of the controversy the truth will spark.

We are in the day when the Breathalyzer, we say, will help police catch the drunk drivers, who must pay. What we need is a "tearalyzer" for the children not growing wiser, those who cry tears of bullets and tears of babies. What will we do for them when all they ask for is a loving friend?

In the class of life these people have been
some of my greatest teachers.

Monica Anthony

Michael Frett

Gary Rhymer

Wayne Hillard

Oprah Winfrey

Zelia Frett

Martin Halpern

Calvin Johnson

Robert Norris

Akim Johnson

Michael Anthony

Jim Clemente

Anna Robles

Kenya Newton

Elton Callwood

Valerye Williams

Marlon Green

Mayjoune Freeman

Medita Wheatley

The Saints at Apostolic Faith Church in Brooklyn NY

The people of the Virgin Islands

Thank You

Life is a class

One of my earliest childhood memories is standing in the mirror singing my heart out to some Michael Jackson song. What I remember is being able to do that with no judgment, no self-hatred, and no hurt from the displeasure of what I saw in the mirror. I missed that innocence that I recall in myself at that moment in time. The gravity of the innocence I had lost was realized fully on the set of The Oprah Winfrey Show. As I was being seated a producer handed me a picture of myself as I looked as a child. The topic of the shows for which I was in attendance was "A two day Oprah show event: 200 Adult Men who were molested come forward" (Those shows aired November 5th and 12th 2010.) I had long put those memories away, but as I sat there and looked around at all those other men who held pictures that reflected the innocence they once knew, it was clear that facing those memories was what we had all come together to do. After all those years of watching Oprah, here I was, a part of one of the most important shows of her career.

Nothing validated this experience for me more than seeing a poster-size picture of me, a replica of the one I held in my hands, posted high up on the stage, as one of eight attached to four separate pillars that stood around Oprah. It was a picture taken by my father similar to the one that adorns the cover of this book. This experience gave me the ultimate feeling of worth and belonging, having grown up being made to feel like my feelings didn't matter. I left that show liberated, empowered, and determined to do whatever I could to share the same message I received while I was there.

I have learned to look at my life as a class. Though I haven't always gotten along with my classmates, en masse. Some I liked, some I loathed, and some I fell in love with; to others I was down right cold. Some I hurt, while others hurt me. Some were forgiving, while others wouldn't let the past be. My experiences with my classmates influenced me. I am more careful now how I allow those experiences to define the kind of person I am growing to be. Especially those experiences I've had as a child, with my classmates who are family. I've learned the lessons that that time defined, and I would have loved to graduate with them, but instead I must leave them behind.

None of us can afford to get stuck in the tragedy of a day, when life has so much more to offer than what any particular experience may portray. Nor can we afford to waste any time with individuals who choose to live in an unproductive and self-destructive way.

My focus has long shifted to creating the kind of life I want to live from the inside out. I believe that our lives are a direct reflection of what our hearts and minds are trying to shout. Rather than entertaining any sort of negativity I seek out those who bring the light with them where ever they go. What life is like when darkness is surrounding me I very well know. I know now how beautiful life is when we are able to see it through the light. Through faith I've expanded my sight. Now I set out to go to a place where I never thought I might. A place where my heart and soul can truly take flight.

I think I've been a better student in the class of life, than I've been in the academic one. What I know is until you realize that life is a class, the learning of its lessons cannot come to pass. For too many this is the truth, they ditch class for most of their youth. They waste time in the halls fooling around, which often leads to time behind bars they can't break down. I've been to detention a couple of times, and I'm glad it didn't lead me to San Quentin for greater crimes.

I know that there is a purpose for all that we as human beings go through. I believe that there is a greater work that we all must do. Our purpose here is to find that thing which we love to do. Even better when that thing helps out another person or two. When you find that thing you most certainly will know, because it will light up your soul all a-glow. Everyone else will know it too, because it will change us as it's changing you.

It's time to come to class. The time we have here is precious don't let it pass. For what a waste that would be, for God to send the world a flower and it's beauty we never get to see. We serve as students and teachers for each other in many ways. So if you are not present the lessons are not as sweet on those days. The blessings are not as deep, and the picture is not as complete, as they would be if you were in your seat.

I've found my purpose and it is changing me. Now I can stand up in class and share these words with you confidently. Now when I look in the mirror I don't hate what I see. I am nurturing a love that's growing deep within me. I fly on the wings of a faith towards greater things to be. I know that this, too, can be your destiny. So I've written these notes in hopes of sharing them with you, because they have meant the world to me. I hope they shine some light for you, on the stony path that life can be.

The End.

Join the community of readers who love this book

Follow us on Twitter:
@LINQBonSale

Like us on Facebook:
www.facebook.com/emancipationofakil

Visit us at
ApoeticLife.com

* 9 7 8 0 9 8 5 6 0 5 5 0 6 *